STRICTLY
MURDER!

A Writer's Guide to Criminal Homicide

Martin Roth

SILES PRESS LOS ANGELES

10 9 8 7 6 5 4 3 2 1

Library of Congress Cataloging in Publication Data

Roth, Martin, 1924–
Strictly murder! : a writer's guide
to criminal homicide / by Martin Roth ; [foreword by Tom Lange].
p cm.
By Martin Roth, with several short chapters written by others.
Includes bibliographical references and filmography.
1. Detective and mystery stories—Authorship.
2. Detective and mystery stories—Handbooks, manuals, etc.
3. Murder—United States–Handbooks, manuals, etc.
4. Homicide—United States—Handbooks, manuals, etc. I. Title.
PN3377.5.D4R595 1998 808.3'872—dc21 98-1187

ISBN: 1-890085-03-0

Cover design by Wade Lageose, Art Hotel

Printed and bound in the United States of America

SILES PRESS
3624 Shannon Road
Los Angeles, CA 90027

To my better half, Marjorie, and to the rest of my family, Lissa, Michelle, Bob, Bruce, Randy, and Tony, I dedicate this book with all my love.

CONTENTS

PREFACE by Tom Lange xi

ACKNOWLEDGMENTS xiii

INTRODUCTION xv

STRICTLY MURDER 1
Arrests
Temporary Detention of a Suspect
Warrants

MURDER IN THE FIRST 4
Where Are We Now?

GLOSSARY 7

THE MANY CAUSES OF DEATH 12

OUTSTANDING MURDER CASES 14

MURDER VERSUS SUICIDE 20

HOMICIDE: PREFACE by Jerry Laird 23

HOMICIDE 25

CRIMINAL HOMICIDE 27
Murder One

Murder in the Second Degree
Voluntary Manslaughter
Mitigating Circumstances
Manslaughter

Female Murderers 31

Contract Killers 32

Organized Crime 34

Domestic Murders 40
Premeditated Spousal Murders

Kids Who Kill & Killers of Kids 42
Killers of Kids
Kids Killing Kids (and Adults)

Serial Killers 46
The Female Serial Killer

Sex & Murder 51

The Act of Terrorism: Preface by Dr. Stephen Sloan 52

Terrorism 55

Terrorism: Q & A 58

Cults That Kill: Preface by Dr. Hannah Evans 62

Cults and Sects 63
The Occult Versus the Cult

Victims 65
Examining and Identifying the Victim

Homicide Photographs 68

MURDER WEAPONS & THE MEANS TO MURDER 73
Strangling and Hanging
Shooting
Asphyxiation
Stabbing, Cutting, Hacking
Blunt Trauma
Other Weapons and Means
A Note to Writers

THE MURDER INVESTIGATION 77
The Five "W"s

MOTIVES FOR MURDER 79

LAW ENFORCEMENT 87

HITS: HOMICIDE INVESTIGATION & TRACKING SYSTEM 89

TIPS FROM A TOP INVESTIGATOR 91
In the Event the Crime Appears to Have Been Committed Outdoors
In the Event the Victim's Body Has Been Disfigured, Altered, or Is Just Skeletal Remains

THE PROFILER 95
A Profiler Checklist

THE PRIVATE INVESTIGATOR & BOUNTY HUNTERS 99
The Life of the TV, Film and Fiction Private Eye Is Murder!
Bounty Hunters

THE HOMICIDE INVESTIGATION: THE CRIME SCENE 103
Types of Homicide

THE MURDER BOOK 107

THE CRIME LAB: PREFACE by Barry Fisher 149

The Crime Lab (The Silent Witness) 152
Crime Lab Equipment for Crime Scene Examination

Crime Lab Photographs 160

Crime Lab: Q & A 165

The Medical Examiner 171
The Post Mortem: The Autopsy
Examination Points for a Complete Autopsy

The Ongoing Investigation 174

Homicide: Q & A 175

The District Attorney & the Prosecutor 186
Filing

The Defendant & the Counsel for the Defense 188

The Courtroom 189
The Arraignment
The Preliminary Hearing
The Trial
Juvenile Justice
The Insanity Defense
The Trial Underway
The Verdict
The Penalty Phase
The Appeal

Courtroom: Q & A 193

The Death Watch 195

Murders That Out 197

Suggested Films 207

PREFACE

By Tom Lange, Los Angeles Police Department,
Homicide Special Section, Retired
(Lead Detective on the O.J. Simpson Case)

Many times I have read newspaper accounts of high-profile murder cases I had been intimately involved with and wondered what case the reporter was writing about. We all realize the need to tell a good story, to make it interesting, but where was the *credibility*? This reporting could be the stuff of a good "whodunit," even when the facts were readily apparent.

Case in point: the Simpson investigation and subsequent trial. In homicide parlance, the Simpson case was *a turkey on a platter* to prosecute. *A no-brainer, a smoking gun* (or, in this instance, *a dripping knife*). Instead, we have "The Trial of the Century." The media, legitimate and otherwise, chose to embellish on conjecture and lend a certain perceived veracity to defense arguments about police conspiracy and bungling. It didn't matter that one would not comport with the other. It only mattered that the story had conflict. Any writer realizes that conflict is an important element of a story, but in the Simpson case, was it reality? Did these nefarious theories, with no basis in fact, make sense in a case that had no exculpatory evidence? Or was the lack of that evidence the motive behind the theories?

Simpson is a glaring example of reporting gone wild, reporting out of control. No facts, no validity. Only sensation. There have been many "lesser" cases presented in the media just as inaccurately. If writers are to lend validity to a particular story, they should familiarize themselves with such things as proper police procedure, terminology, proven and accepted investigative methods, and plain common sense. All too often we see dramatic license taken to unbelievable levels. We read of the homicide cop who internalizes every nuance of the investigation to the extent that it totally consumes him or her. These things do happen, but very seldom. Even then the situation is never as grave as portrayed, but we have the *conflict.* Reality is not always interesting, but it is reality.

In *Strictly Murder*, Martin Roth, an established writer and producer of numerous crime-based television shows, bridges reality with fantasy. This educational guide serves to assist the television or fiction writer with *accurately* described police investigative practices. It is also a fascinating study of that which grips us all . . . *murder.*

Acknowledgments

Assembling the information for this book was a monumental task that required the assistance and the expertise of a number of individuals and law enforcement agencies who unselfishly gave of their time and professional experience. I wish to express my thanks and sincere appreciation to each and everyone of them, and I humbly apologize to anyone I might have inadvertently omitted.

To Los Angeles County Sheriff Sherman Block, who helped open a lot of doors; Barry A. J. Fisher, Chief of the Los Angeles County Sheriff's Criminalistics Laboratory; Detective Tom Lange, Los Angeles Police Department Homicide Special Section, Retired; Sergeant Rey Verdugo, Robbery/Homicide Bureau, Los Angeles County Sheriff's Department; Detective Mike Robinson and Detective Mike Bumcrot, Robbery/Homicide Bureau, Los Angeles County Sheriff's Department; Sergeant Bob Furtak, San Diego Police Department; Dr. Hannah Evans, Ph.D., criminal and cult expert; The Los Angeles County District Attorney's Office; The United States Department of Justice; The Federal Bureau of Investigation; Dr. Steven Sloan, Professor of Political Science at The University of Oklahoma and adviser to the White House on terrorism; Detective Jerry Laird, Robbery/Homicide, Riverside County, California, Retired; Sergeant Barry Perrou in command of the Los Angeles County Sheriff's Crisis Negotiations Team; James J. Docherty, New York Police Department and Los Angeles Police Department, Retired; Richard Freedman, Private Investigator; John T. Lynch, Private Investigator; The Internet Crimewriters Network (crimewriters.com/Crime); Randy E. Gibson,

Forensic Scientist, San Diego Police Department; and Sergeant Tom Monahan, Las Vegas Metro Police Department, Retired; all of whom gave of their expertise in helping to provide much of the information contained herein regarding the subject of murder.

Introduction

If one carefully examines the television news, checks the weekly listings of television movies and episodic dramas, and glances at the movie ads, the odds are good that more than fifty percent of both the news and the fictional world of TV and film deal with cold-blooded murder.

Why?

Because the public is fascinated with the subject. The public is deeply intrigued with the whys and wherefores of violence. The public craves nightmarish violence—as long as it happens elsewhere and to someone we don't know. Therefore, we, the writers—news writers, non-fiction writers, fiction writers, television and film writers—fulfill that craving.

Although the twentieth century has become known as the "Age of Violence," it may be but a preface to what is to come in the twenty-first century, as violence and especially murder almost become a way of life for modern man. Where wars were once fought on battlefields, they are now fought on the streets of our cities and in the homes and in the schools and on the playgrounds in which our families live and work and play.

Murder has become the number one sport for both killers and spectators. An abundance of murders and murderers exists to read about and to write about. There are murderous street gangsters; killers associated with organized crime; serial killers; spousal, child, and parent abusers who kill; robbers, rapists, terrorists, and racists who kill; cult leaders and cult members who kill; angry people who seek murderous revenge against all who stand in their way; and those who kill for the sheer thrill of it. *Strictly Murder* will explore all of these killers and the law enforcement people who attempt to bring them to justice.

⁕ ⁕ ⁕ ⁕ ⁕

I hope that *Strictly Murder*'s Q & A sections will cover some of the questions you've asked yourself but didn't know where to turn to find the answers. These sections are made up of questions posed to me and to homicide officers, crime scene technicians, criminalists and forensic specialists, prosecutors and defense counsel, and law enforcement personnel with whom I have worked during the forty-odd years of my career as a crime writer. The answers these professionals provide are based on their expertise and personal experiences.

Also included in this book are interviews with homicide officers who have dealt with and still do deal with death and killers on a daily basis. Their thoughts on the subject of murder offer insights into their lives not only as law enforcement officers but also as people who, perhaps, have seen too much violence.

In addition to those elements mentioned above, I've included a Glossary of terms that is as up-to-date as possible and a complete Murder Book—the collection of all the reports and information obtained in a real-life murder case that has now been solved and concluded. If you are writing about homicide, this book will help you to understand various aspects of murder, the murderer, the victim, and the investigation process, so that you may be more factual in what you portray on the screen or on the pages in your novel.

A Few Words of Warning

Although I have attempted to put together a well-researched book dealing with the various aspects of murder, the reader must realize that there is no one bible for all murder investigations. Many specific aspects of a murder investigation depend on the locality of the law enforcement agency and the jurisdictions that are involved in the investigation. Even the official titles of those involved in an investigation may differ from city to city and state to state. The person investigating a murder may be a detective or an investigator. And detectives and investigators have different ranks, depending on the city in which they work. The homicide investigating section may be called Robbery/Homicide, Detective Division, Homicide Squad, Major Crimes Squad, Investigative Section, etc. Those attending the crime scene may be called criminalists, forensic specialists, technicians, etc.

The point is, the titles used in this book are generic, so you, as a writer, should always check with the appropriate agencies for the proper names and titles when you are writing about a specific city or state. Of course, if your city is a mythical one, the choice is yours, but at the same time, you don't want the credibility of your work to be challenged. Check out these names and titles before you go into print or production.

After reading *Strictly Murder*, I'm sure that you will have some questions that remain unanswered, some information that you still desire. Some murder cases don't provide us with all of the answers to why and how the murder occurred. But to cite an old adage, "seek and ye shall find." If this book just helps you to become more aware of what can occur, then it will have aided you in your writing and in your understanding of what is murder. I have included suggested reading for further research. If you don't find what you're looking for here, look there.

Strictly Murder

It's amazing how many people hear the word "homicide" and immediately assume it to mean "murder." But homicide only means "the taking of a human life."

There are two types of homicides: innocent, due to natural causes or as the result of a legitimate accident, and criminal. It is the job of the Homicide Bureau and its investigators to determine if death was (1) a suicide, (2) an excusable or justifiable homicide, or (3) a criminal homicide. Most criminal homicides are fairly evident; however, some criminal homicides can be made to look innocent or natural.

When a pathologist performing an autopsy discovers something suspicious about the deceased, murder is suspected and a criminal homicide investigation begins. Sometimes, the deceased appears to have died a natural death or died at his or her own hands. But if the investigator suspects it is neither a natural death nor a suicide, the results of the autopsy will show if there is truly a reason to suspect a criminal homicide.

The U.S. Justice Department's National Institute of Justice estimates that, depending on residence, lifestyle, occupation, and socioeconomic status, the majority of criminal homicide victims are between the ages of fifteen and thirty-five. People surviving past the age of thirty-five have a distinctly smaller chance of falling victim to a criminal homicide. Statistics show that the annual chance of becoming a criminal homicide victim is 1 in 10,200; in a lifetime, the chances are 1 in 151.

ARRESTS

Although the 5th Amendment protects a citizens from self-incrimination, the 6th Amendment states that police cannot interview a defendant without his lawyer present, and the Supreme Court ruled (in the Miranda case) more than three decades ago that police must inform a suspect that he or she has the right to remain silent and the right to counsel before being interrogated—*but there is a loophole!* Before arresting a suspect, detectives are free to detain and question the suspect without reading the suspect his or her Miranda Rights. In other words, as long as the suspect has not been arrested, it is perfectly legal for the police to question that person as long as he or she is not deprived of his or her civil rights. Should the interrogating officer lead the suspect to believe that he or she is not free to go, then the 5th Amendment and Miranda come into play.

TEMPORARY DETENTION OF A SUSPECT

Should an officer doing an interrogation have reason to believe that the individual being interrogated is a viable and likely suspect, the officer may detain the suspect (in most cases between forty-eight and seventy-two hours) without making a formal arrest.

The term "probable cause" stems from our Constitution's 4th Amendment, which states that "the right of the people shall be secure in their persons against unreasonable search and seizure shall not be violated, and no warrants shall be issued without probable cause." In other words, hunches, guesses, and assumptions don't count. The arresting officer MUST have some evidence linking an individual to a crime, even if such evidence is not proof of the suspect having committed the crime. Such evidence need not be found by personal observation but can come from a tip, a witness, an informer, or a victim.

WARRANTS

An arrest made *without a warrant* requires the arresting officer to identify himself or herself, announce his or her intention to make the arrest, identify the crime that the suspect is being arrested for and read the suspect his or her Miranda rights.

Should a police office suspect that a crime has been committed on private property, he or she must secure permission to enter the property from the owner or manager of the property unless probable cause has been established, in which case the officer could request a warrant to enter the premises from a judge.

The conditions under which an officer may search a subject, a premises, a vehicle belonging to a suspect, etc., are subject to many legal requirements regarding search and seizure. It is essential that you check with the local authorities of the city and state that you are writing about to determine what the local legal requirements are.

MURDER IN THE FIRST

When was the first murder committed? Probably sometime after Adam and Eve met if statistics are correct and domestic violence is the precursor to murder. But leaving the bible aside, from the time of the first Homo sapiens, murder flourished, as evidenced by archeological discoveries of many skulls that appear to have been fractured as a direct result of blunt trauma, i.e., cavemen who were hit over the head by a rock or club, probably as a result of a struggle for power or food.

Then, as the world became more populated, cannibalism appeared and, as man came to believe in spirits and gods, religious sacrifice of humans were performed in a variety of rituals that could easily be construed as murder.

Let's face it: Things didn't get much better as history progressed. Kings and queens, emperors and empresses were always having someone beheaded or poisoned, usually for political reasons. And during the fourteenth and fifteenth centuries, it was recorded that Gilles de Rias, a non-political killer, enjoyed killing sprees, especially sexually assaulting and then killing young children (a form of murder that appears to have lasted down through the centuries and is prominent today).

And, although he has become somewhat of a mythical character thanks to Bram Stoker, there actually was a Dracula (his full name was Vlad Tepes Dracula), a fifteenth-century Rumanian prince who delighted in mass murders, especially in impaling and burning alive hundreds of Saxon merchants.

Murders or homicides soon became mass murders as genocide under the guise of racial or religious cleansing became the order of the day, followed closely by economic bigotry as a principal motive. Mass killings escalated from the eleventh through the sixteenth century, and numerous murders were committed in the name of the Christian faith, beginning with The Crusades, continuing through the Spanish Inquisition, and culminating in witch hunts in both England and the United States. Of course, we must not fail to include Adolph Hitler and Nazi Germany in the twentieth century for the mass murders of more than six million men, women, and children, the majority of whom were Jewish.

⟩ ⟩ ⟩ ⟩ ⟩

If you are concerned today about ample police protection, you should know that our ancestors had none until the year 1753, when a writer (yes, one of us) by the name of Henry Fielding (he wrote *Tom Jones*) began writing barbed attacks on the Warpole government and organized a non-governmental group called the Bow Street Runners. Before 1753, the British had their sheriffs and other nations around the world had one individual who supposedly enforced the law of his king or queen, but organized police forces were a long way off, primarily because most people distrusted that kind of authority.

It was not until the early 1800s that law and order began to take hold with the U.K. and in the United States (with local sheriffs and their posses in the old west). The U.S. Marshal, however, is actually the oldest law enforcement agency in the U.S., which was followed by the Postal Inspectors because of the many mail robberies that were committed against the stage coaches and the trains racing west. Eventually, the railroads would form their own police department.

In 1829, the British statesman Sir Robert Peel organized a police force that began to protect British citizens, but across the ocean, it wasn't until 1884 that the great city of New York established its first police department.

WHERE ARE WE NOW?

Today, we have city or metropolitan police, the District Attorney's Office, the County Sheriff's Department, the Highway Patrol, the Border Patrol, the Life Guard Service, the Harbor Patrol, the State Police, and an untold number of other law enforcement agencies operating out of the Federal Government's Department of Justice, the Treasury Department, The Defense Department, and various branches of the military.

It should be noted, however, that federal agencies seldom become involved in criminal homicide investigation, the one major exception being the military, which conducts its own murder investigations, trials, prisons, and executions.

Generally, criminal homicide investigations are handled by the local police department or the sheriff's department, depending upon the jurisdiction in which the homicide occurred.

With the exception of very small towns, most local law enforcement agencies are well equipped or have access to unbelievable modern technologies to assist them in solving murders and bringing the killer to justice. Unfortunately, despite the latest technologies available in our rapidly growing, computerized world, the army of criminals, terrorists, and violent cults continues to grow, and, sadly, the criminals are outgunning the law enforcement agencies.

Combine these criminals with the mentally unbalanced who walk our streets, and our overcrowded, under-funded prisons, and a too-liberal justice system that puts all sorts of felons back on the streets with a mere slap on the wrist, and it is apparent why criminals seem to be getting the upper hand in our war against crime and murder.

Of course, not every homicide begins with murderous intent. Murders committed during the course of robberies, rapes, kidnappings, blackmailings, burglaries, and a hundred other crimes do not necessarily begin as premeditated murder. But let a drug bust go wrong, a gang war erupt, a robbery victim be too slow to respond to the robber's demand, an intended victim reach for a weapon to defend himself, a rape victim struggle too hard, and you can almost bank on a killing occurring.

The statistics are appalling. Our country—the whole world for that matter—appears to be filled with anger, hate, bigotry, greed, lust, and a complete and utter disregard for human life.

GLOSSARY

Although many basic words, terms, and expressions are used in association with murder and murder investigations, every law enforcement agency seems to have developed some of its own terminology. For example, the N.Y.P.D. will call the individual who committed a crime "the perp," meaning the perpetrator, whereas the L.A.P.D. will to refer to that person as "the suspect."

I've endeavored to put together a Glossary of many of these murder-related terms so that when you read the Q & A sections of this book, you won't have to stop and ask, "What's that mean?"

AAG: Assistant Attorney General.
After hair: Chasing women for sexual purposes.
Attitude adjuster: Policeman's baton.
Bag and tag: Collecting crime scene evidence and identifying it.
Bag it: Bag the hands and feet to protect prints.
B & D: Bondage and discipline.
Bleeder: Extortionist, blackmailer.
Bone bender: Physician.
Boyfriend-girlfriend thing: A romantic dispute turned homicidal.
Boxed on the table: Died on the operating table.
Burrhead: A prison inmate, usually a black person.
Buzzer: Police shield.
Blunt force: Use of a heavy instrument or club, kicking, or hitting with a vehicle, etc.
Capos: Mafia lieutenants.
CATCH: Computer Assisted Terminal Criminal Hunt.

Chicken hawk: Child molester.
Collar: Arrest.
Contract: An order to have someone killed.
Corpus delecti: The body of evidence.
CSU: Crime Scene Unit.
DB: Dead body.
DCDS: Deceased confirmed dead at the scene.
DEV: Deviant, pervert.
DD: Dying declaration.
DNA: Deoxyribonucleic acid blood-test, which can identify an individual bearing the same properties in their blood as the blood that may have been found at a homicide scene.
DOJ: Department of Justice.
D.O.A.: Dead on arrival.
Do the dog: To wander around crime scene as a detective not on the case.
Dragon blood: Red fingerprint powder.
Dropped the dime: Talked, revealed information on someone or about something that happened.
Drop gun: A gun, usually confiscated from a criminal, that is carried by a police officer to plant at a crime scene to justify a dubious shooting.
Family album: A loose-leaf notebook of 8x10 murder-scene photos.
Fed sled: Federal vehicle.
Felo-de-se: One who commits suicide, a felony against one's self.
Fink: Stool pigeon, informant
Flake: Frame, set up. (A Flake: A phony.)
Floater: Body recovered from water.
Flyer: Individual who jumped or was pushed out of a window or off a rooftop.
Freelance enforcer: A hired gun who is not a member of a mob, the Mafia, or a gang.
Frontman/stand-in: Person who takes the rap for a higher up.
Gloves: Latex gloves worn by homicide investigators and members of the CSR so as not to contaminate the CS. Also used to protect officers

and CSU personnel from touching blood that might contain the HIV virus.

Go down: Take place.

Grounder: An easy case to wrap up.

Hit man: Hired killer who works on a "contract."

Homeboy: Someone from the neighborhood.

In clothes: A police officer out of uniform.

Jane Doe: Unidentified female body.

Jerking the chains: Law enforcement officers using whatever knowledge they have on a criminal to get his or her cooperation.

John Doe: Unidentified male body.

Juan Doe: Unidentified Latino body.

Landline: A call made by a police officer on a pay phone in place of a car radio.

Latent print: Print that is not visible to the naked eye, but found by using dusting powder.

Lividity: Part of the body where the blood settles after death.

Lying-in-wait: Concealment that determines premeditation and planning by a perpetrator prior to committing a murder.

Make: Identify (Also used when becoming a member of a Mafia family).

Megabitch: Real bad female.

Mens rea: Criminal intent.

Mom killer: Killer of old ladies.

Paper-hanger: Person who writes bad checks.

Patsy: A detective's gold shield.

Perp: Perpetrator.

Piece: Gun.

Pin: Identify a lifestyle.

Pissing backwards: A witness on the witness stand presenting testimony that is contrary to the story that witness told to the police.

Post: Autopsy or post-mortem.

Rabbi: High-ranking police officer who has taken a lower ranked officer under his wing.

Recorder: Police officer who is responsible for recording all visitors to a crime scene.

Ripe: A non-buried homicide victim's body that has been decaying for a period of time before being discovered.
Rough-shadowing: Tailing a suspect in such a manner as to harass or apply pressure to the suspect by letting the suspect know that he is being watched.
SAC: Special Agent in Charge of an FBI office.
Secretors: Individuals who carry a group-specific substance in their blood stream, making it possible to determine such body fluids as saliva, semen, urine, tears, perspiration, and nasal secretion.
Shake cards: Police file cards on criminals, suspects, or fugitives currently being tailed or sought or under investigation by police.
Shitcan: Homicide that is unlikely to be solved.
Shooter: Individual who fired a weapon.
Smear: Blood smear that occurs when a bloodstained object is brushed against another article.
Spike: Heroin user's needle.
Splatter: The way the blood falls from a victim. This pattern can be used to determine the position of the victim when he or she was shot.
S.O.L.: Shit out of luck.
Stand-up guy: Individual who is respected for not turning against his or her friends or co-workers.
Steal the bust: Take away credit for an arrest.
Stringer: Freelance reporter.
Stoolie: Individual working for or under pressure from law enforcement to reveal information about a crime or a criminal suspect.
Stonkered: Dead, killed, murdered.
Suit: Detective on the way up, or a higher-ranked officer.
Tag: ID tag placed on a victim's toe. Also, the ID attached to evidence to establish a chain of custody.
Tin: Police officer's shield.
Toss: Pat someone down, frisk someone.
Tommy buster: Rapist.
T.P.O.: Time and place of occurrence.
Tracks: Needle marks on a drug user's body. Also, human footprints and marks made by vehicles and animals.

24-24: The last twenty-four hours of a victim's life.
Un-sub: Unidentified subject.
Up: Being the next detective on call.
Use of a deadly weapon: A term used to presume malice.
Waste: Kill.
Whip: Officer in charge.
VICAP: Violent Criminals Apprehension Program.
Vic: Victim.

THE MANY CAUSES OF DEATH

One of the most important things the homicide investigator must attempt to discover is the cause of death, which can determine if the death was a suicide, an accidental death, or a criminal homicide. (This is not always easy, e.g., should a suicide victim be of the Catholic faith, there is always the possibility that the body was made to look as if the victim had been murdered, because Catholics cannot be buried in hallowed ground if they have committed suicide.)

The Medical Examiner (a licensed pathologist) is the only one to determine the actual cause of death, which may be from:

- drowning
- hanging
- strangulation
- asphyxiation
- shooting
- stabbing
- poisoning
- falling from a great height
- blunt trauma
- drug overdose
- beating

Many times, the cause of death determined at the crime scene may differ greatly from the cause of death discovered during the autopsy or post mortem. This could happen because the Medical Examiner Investigator who is sent to the scene is not a doctor or pathologist but a general investigator schooled, as a Crime Scene Medical Investigator, in certain areas, such as determining the apparent cause of death and the approximate time of death. It will take a full postmortem to reveal the actual cause of death. What appeared to be a fatal gunshot or stabbing may actually have been a poisoning.

Outstanding Murder Cases

True murder cases are often more bizarre than fictional ones and, if carefully studied by writers, can often become great stories, films, or novels.

It would take many volumes to describe the truly major, high-profile murder cases of the twentieth century, many of which have been documented in biographies and, in some cases, autobiographies by the killers themselves. Quite a few of their stories have even made it to the big screen, or have been made into movies for television.

I have provided a list of high-profile killers whom you might want to research to make sure that their stories haven't already been told. Even if they have been, these stories might be worth retelling if you can come up with new, unique spins on them. But I suggest you first find out if the stories that interest you have been done to death (pardon the pun). Of course, there's always the possibility of using the m.o. (modus operandi) of a high-profile killer. Just alter the character in some fashion and use the main plotline with some adjustments to develop a fictional story based on a true one.

Naturally, it's impossible to offer a sizable portion of information on all of these killers, but here are a few examples:

One of the most famous cases did not begin with a premeditated murder. It began with a kidnapping—one of the most famous kidnappings of all time, and of the offspring of one of the most famous men of our time, Charles Lindbergh.

Lindbergh's child, a 20-month-old, beautiful, blonde, curly haired boy, disappeared from the Lindbergh home in Hopewell, New Jersey, on March 1, 1932, between the hours of 8:00 and 10:00 P.M. All that Lindbergh heard while reading in his downstairs library was a sharp, cracking sound—then silence. Lindbergh went back to his book. A short time later, the baby's nurse, Betty Gow, paid a visit to the nursery and discovered the empty crib. Minutes later, the police were on their way, having been summoned by the family butler while Lindbergh grabbed a searchlight and a Springfield rifle and went out into the night, hoping to find the kidnapper and the child. The only clues that were found were indistinct footprints, as if the kidnapper's shoes had been bound up in cloth, and a crude ladder in sections, one of the steps having been broken (the sharp crack the Colonel had heard?). The final clue was a ransom note that boasted quite a few misspellings.

Thus began the search for the Lindbergh baby, which ended on May 12, almost two and half months after the kidnapping, when a truck driver named William Allen stumbled across a shallow, leaf-covered grave while walking in the woods only a few miles from Colonel Lindbergh's home. The baby had been dead since the night he had been taken, his death occurring from severe injuries to the head.

The main clue that eventually brought the kidnapper/murderer Bruno Hauptmann to justice was discovered not by a detective but by Arthur Koehler, a member of the U.S. Forestry Service, who traced the source of the cheap and ordinary pieces of wood the kidnapper used to build the ladder that he used climbed up to the Lindbergh's second-floor nursery and back down with the baby.

Koehler spent eighteen months tracking down the lumberyard where the wood was purchased. This became one of the major pieces of evidence against Hauptmann when he was eventually caught. But what brought about the capture of the kidnapper/murderer was, believe it or not, the international monetary crisis that caused President Roosevelt to abandon the gold standard, which in turn revealed Hauptmann, who had collected most of the ransom money in gold certificates, when he attempted to use those gold certificates to purchase gasoline for his car. A twist that I doubt most writers would have ever come up with.

TED BUNDY, who began his chilling killing career as a handsome charmer who had an unlimited number of beautiful young women just panting to be with him, was probably one of the highest-profile serial rapists/killers in history. His urge to kill left a trail of murders behind him so long that the true death toll is unknown to this day, Bundy having taken his secrets with him to his grave.

Theodore Robert Bundy, born in Philadelphia in a home for unwed mothers in 1946, was the illegitimate child of Louise Cowell. At age four he went with his mother to Tacoma, Washington, where she met and married John Bundy.

Self-conscious and oversensitive, he became a thief and a liar at age thirteen, although he did receive good grades in school and eventually went on to attend the University of Washington. There, a startling change came about in Bundy's personality. He left behind his shy behavior and transformed himself into an extremely self-confident young man.

In examining Bundy's life, it's noteworthy that he became infatuated with an attractive young woman named Stephanie Brooks while in his late teens. But Stephanie quickly tired of Bundy's lack of sophistication and dumped him. He was deeply affected by this breakup and, while studying law at the University of Pudget Sound, he began toying around with petty crime. Around this same time, he and Stephanie met again, and now the roles were reversed. Stephanie found that Bundy had matured and she sought his company, but now Bundy dumped her. The revenge he got from dumping her seemed to trigger a sense of power and confidence in Bundy, and he embarked on life of rape and murder. Bundy's crime spree, if his long string of rapes and murders could be called a spree, began sometime in or around October 1974.

Among the numerous young women he charmed to death were 21-year-old Lynda Ann Healy, 19-year-old Donna Gail Manson, 18-year-old Susan Rancourt, 22-year-old Roberta Parks, 22-year-old Brenda Ball, 8-year-old Georgann Hawkins, 23-year-old Janice Ott, 19-year-old Denise Naslund, 17-year-old Debbie Kent, 17-year-old Melissa Smith, 17-year-old Laura Aime, 16-year-old Nancy Wilcox, and 23-year-old Caryn Campell. A young woman named Carol DaRonch was the only one of his sexually assaulted victims who escaped from Bundy, and she later identified him as her attacker.

Arrested and charged as the brutal and sadistic sex killer he was, Bundy managed to escape from the second-floor window of the courthouse where he was to be tried, but was captured six days later.

A series of credit card receipts were, in essence, the first evidence that led police to suspect Ted Bundy as the multiple sex killer they were seeking. He was a cocky young man who managed to elude the police for a long period of time and even acted as his own lawyer when facing the death sentence. Bundy's story is a fascinating one, but much too long a tale to tell here. He was put to death in the execution chamber at Starke Prison, Florida, on January 24, 1989, while crowds outside the prison chanted, "Fry Bundy." The story goes that the ever-cocky Bundy died with a self-satisfied smirk on his face.

DAVID BERKOWITZ was the "Son of Sam" killer (1976-77) who selected his victims, who were primarily young, single, white, middle-class women, to ensure major press coverage.

CHARLES MANSON, a mentally unbalanced cult leader, is responsible for the thrill killing of pregnant Sharon Tate and everyone else in her house on that day. His band of killers, made up mainly of young female followers, not only killed everyone in cold blood but delighted in mutilating their bodies.

CHARLES WHITMAN is remembered for what has become known as The Texas Tower Massacre. Whitman was a mass murderer (not a serial killer) who took up a position in a university tower and indiscriminately mowed down anyone who came into sights of his high-powered rifle.

DR. SAM SHEPHERD was accused of murdering his wife while she was in bed. He was tried (mainly by the press), found guilty, and sent to prison. He was released years later, and after his release his innocence of the murder was discovered.

WILLIAM HEIRENS was dubbed "The Lipstick Killer" in 1945

because, after killing Frances Brown in her apartment in her residential hotel, he scrawled in lipstick across the top of her bed, "For God's sake catch me before I kill more. I cannot control myself."

Considered to suffer from the Jekyll/Hyde Syndrome, Heirens began his killing career at age sixteen, after having been sent to a variety of correctional facilities for burglary. At the time, the police failed to take note that the burglaries were, in a sense, sexually motivated—the young boy was stealing women's panties.

His first murder was not premeditated, but came as the result of being interrupted while in the process of committing a burglary. The police believe his subsequent murder of Josephine Ross, a 45-year-old divorcee, was premeditated.

In January of 1946, Heirens kidnapped 6-year-old Suzanne Degan, leaving behind a ransom note demanding $20,000. However, Heirens had already strangled the child, dismembered her body, washed the pieces of her body (as he had with each of his previous victims), and disposed of the body parts. In June of 1946, Heirens was taken into custody, where he claimed that the crimes he was accused of were committed by a man named George, Heirens' second personality who took over Heirens in the true Jekyll-and-Hyde tradition. Heirens or George or both were sentenced to three consecutive life terms.

Other famous cases you might want to read up on:

Richard Ramirez: "The Night Stalker"
Kenneth Bianchi: "The Hillside Strangler"
Albert Fish: "The Cannibal Killer"
Albert Desalvo: "The Boston Strangler"
Ma and William Bender: "The Bloody Benders"
Edmund Kemper: "The Co-Ed Killer"
Wayne Kearney: "The Trash-Bag Murders"
Wayne Williams: "The Atlanta Child Murders"
Jeffrey Dahmer: "The Mass-Mutilation Murders"
Richard Kuhlinski: "The Ice Man Murders"
Nanny Hazel Doss: "The Husband Killer"
Charles Starkweather and Caril Fugate: "They Loved to Kill!"

SUGGESTED READING

The Psychology of Strange Killers, James Melvin Reinhardt, Charles C. Thomas Publishing, Springfield, IL.
The Murderer and his Victim, John M. McDonald, Charles C. Thomas Publishing

MURDER VERSUS SUICIDE

The following rules pretty much determine that a body that has been discovered is that of a victim of murder rather than of suicide.

You can be sure that the victim has met with foul play if . . .

DEATH BY FIREARM: (a) there is no weapon, (b) a weapon is present but has no prints on it, (c) the victim was shot in the back, (d) the victim was shot on the opposite side of his or her body, (e) the victim was shot from a distance longer than length of his or her arm, (f) there are multiple shot wounds, (g) there are signs of a struggle, (h) there is no suicide note.

DEATH BY DROWNING: (a) there are signs of a struggle, (b) the post reveals no sign of water in the lungs, (c) the victim was bound, (d) the victim couldn't swim and avoided water, (e) the victim was discovered in very shallow water.

DEATH BY STABBING: (a) there is no weapon at the scene, (b) there are no prints on the knife, (c) the wound is in the back or the opposite side of the right/left-handed person, (d) there are defensive cuts present on the victim.

DEATH BY HANGING OR STRANGLING: (a) there is a straight bruise around neck, (b) there is no bruise and victim was already dead.

DEATH BY POISON: Although, due to an odor given off by a body or due to a body's skin discoloration, outward appearance indicates that the victim died by poisoning, it is extremely difficult to determine whether the poison was self-induced or induced by another party unless: (a) the food or drink taken by the victim contained a poison that would arouse suspicion of foul play; (b) the poison was induced by injection, which is hardly the way a victim would bring about his or her own death; (c) the poison was induced in some strange manner, such as by a poisonous snake or insect in a location where such a reptile or insect would not normally be found; (d) poisonous fumes were discovered that were of a foreign substance or gas as opposed to a commercial gas used for heating or cooking. And even in this event, an investigator would attempt to discover whether the victim accidentally inhaled the fumes, was seeking to end his or her own life by inhaling the fumes, or was assaulted and left unconscious to breath the poisonous air.

DEATH BY SUFFOCATION: Although it is entirely possible for a victim to suffocate himself by placing a plastic bag over his head, it is highly unlikely because of the normal human reflex to gasp for air. If the death was indeed a suicide, the victim would unquestionably have had to have drugged himself first in order to become unconscious and surrender to the normal human impulse for air. This, however, does not rule out the possibility that, in a criminal homicide, the victim was drugged prior to suffocation or was somehow rendered unconscious prior to suffocation.

MURDERERS AND WAYS TO MURDER

Just as there is an almost unlimited number of ways and means to murder someone, there is an almost unlimited number of types of murderers:

The person who kills for the sheer thrill of killing.

The passive/aggressive killer who remains passive, controlling his or her anger and desire for aggression and revenge until the day that person explodes into violence.

The killer who kills while under the influence of drugs or alcohol.

The various types of serial killers.

The compulsive killer who cannot control himself or herself from killing.

The impulsive killer who suffers from severe impulsion.

The robber, burglar, rapist, terrorist, arsonist, racist, kidnapper who kills without regard for human life.

The mass murderer who needs to kill in large numbers.

The mercy killer who believes in murder as a means to put people out of their misery.

The moralistic or cause killer who cares little for human life while trying to advance his or her moralistic or cause-related issues.

The professional hit man who is "contracted" to kill.

Those interested in United States statistics regarding murder, including race, age, urban or suburban murders, juveniles, organized crime and street-gang killings, should contact the National Institute of Justice of the Department of Justice, Office of Justice Programs, Bureau of Justice Statistics, Box 6000, Rockville, MD 20850, 800-732-3277 (or the NCJRS Worldwide Web page at http://ncjrs.aspensys.com:81/ncjrshome.html) for the specific information you need.

Homicide: Preface

By Jerry Laird, former Riverside County Homicide Investigator

Jerry Laird has spent more than twenty-six years "on the job," and here he offers a variety of information regarding the responsibilities of those involved in a homicide crime-scene investigation.

A Homicide Team should consist of:

(a) A senior supervisor with a solid background in criminal investigation (ten years).

(b) A senior or pair of lead detectives whose responsibility is to direct other team members while at the crime scene as to the collection and preservation of evidence, the potential identification of the suspect(s), and to assist the local district attorney's office with the prosecution once the suspect has been apprehended.

(c) A pair of investigators are assigned to work with the crime-scene sketch artist and photographers (Polaroid, 35mm, and video if available). Polaroid shots are especially helpful in locating evidence not readily seen by the human eye and are used to help determine what is necessary from forensic personnel.

(d) A pair of investigators are assigned to the bag-and-tag part of the investigation.

(e) An officer assigned to record everyone entering and leaving the crime scene. All individuals who come upon the crime scene are required to write a report on his or her activities at the scene.

Blood items, or those containing blood samples, should never be placed in plastic bags or containers other than a glass container, with the collection instrument. A control sample should be taken from the same area and also placed in a glass container. All evidentiary material and blood samples should be marked with the collector's initials, along with date and time.

The location of evidentiary items should be triangulated for diagram purposes. Example: Bladed weapon, silver in color blade area, brown in color handle, containing reddish brown stains on the blade, 7' east of the west #1 bedroom wall and 11'6" south of north #1 bedroom.

Having a representative from the local prosecutor's office on scene so that he or she can get a feel of the scene and the collection of evidence needed for prosecution is highly desirable. He or she can also assist in preparing search warrants, should they be needed, or a "Ramey" warrant, should it be needed for a person.

Homicide

There is homicide and then there is "criminal" homicide. Homicide is the taking of a human life, which could be accidental, negligent, reckless, vehicular, excusable, or justifiable.

An *accidental* homicide means exactly what it implies: The homicide was not meant to happen, there was no intent, premeditation, malice, or motive. The individual who committed the homicide was not under the influence of drugs or alcohol and was in full possession of his or her faculties. If the accident was not due to negligence on the part of the individual who committed the homicide, it would then be considered *excusable.*

The homicide would be considered to be *justifiable* if the individual who committed the homicide was doing it under lawful authority as a law enforcement officer and was empowered to commit the homicide under legally prescribed conditions; if the individual was a soldier who killed the enemy during a time of war; if an innocent individual was defending his or her own life or believed his or her life was actually being threatened and was in immediate danger of being harmed or killed; if an innocent individual commits homicide to protect or defend the life of another whose life is obviously in jeopardy at that precise time.

Most justifiable homicides occur in urban areas, with the number of justifiable homicides fairly split between citizens and law enforcement officers. The weapon most commonly used in a justifiable killing is a firearm, in most cases a handgun.

The majority of justifiable homicides are committed by ordinary citizens who are protecting themselves or their families during a burglary or theft. The second most common reason is in defense of an assault upon oneself or another innocent person.

The largest number of victims of justifiable homicide are males.

Female citizens are more likely to justifiably kill someone they know rather than a stranger, and that person is usually a male.

Whenever a police officer fires his weapon and wounds or kills another human being, an automatic investigation of the "officer involved shooting" is launched to determine if the shots fired by the officer were within the law and that the officer had no other legal recourse but to fire his or her weapon at the suspect.

For example, an officer responding to a robbery sees a suspect emerge from a store that was robbed. His first responsibility when drawing his weapon is to order the suspect to halt, identify himself or herself as a police officer, then order the suspect to drop his weapon, raise his hands above his head, and get down on his knees, face down as the officer approaches the suspect. Should the suspect not respond as ordered and it is apparent that the suspect is going to fire a weapon at the officer, the officer is empowered to fire at the suspect. This then would be considered justifiable homicide. But let us say that the officer only thought he or she saw a weapon in the suspect's hand and the suspect did not actually have a weapon—it might not be a justifiable shooting. Unless the suspect draws a weapon or appears to be in the act of drawing a weapon, the shooting could be questionable. Now let us assume that that same robber came out of the store and the police officer identified himself and, as the robber appeared to run or turn, the officer fired and killed the robber. Then the officer approaches the body of the robber, only to find that the robber did not have a weapon. That shooting would not be justifiable. That is a situation where a "drop gun" could easily come into play: The officer who did the shooting takes a small handgun (non-issued) that he carries (usually ankle-strapped) and places it in the dead robber's hand. The officer then tells the investigating officer that the suspect drew on him and he had no alternative but to fire at the suspect. It's done time and time again. But who can really blame that officer when he or she has to decide whether or not to fire at a suspect in a fraction of a second?

Criminal Homicide

Criminal homicide is not accidental, excusable, or justifiable.

Cases where death occurs from actions that are clearly negligent, such as a parent leaving a child in or under conditions that could cause the child's death, or where an individual shows wanton disregard for human life, a "reckless homicide," would fall into the category of a criminal homicide.

The majority of criminal homicides result from malice aforethought, with the full intent to take a human life for felonious reasons. In essence, murder is homicide with malice. Malice can be directed at an individual, a group, or the entire world. The main question is the definition of "malice."

What does malice actually mean? Hate, ill will? As a matter of semantics, I suppose it would imply that. However, hate and ill will are merely states of mind, while the legal definition of malice constitutes a life-threatening state of mind, which in turn means that the individual committing homicide with malice is committing the act without excuse, justification, or any mitigating circumstances. With an excuse or a justification, homicide is not considered to be criminal. If there were mitigating circumstances (a legitimate explanation that shows no malice), the charge of murder might be lowered to that of voluntary manslaughter.

Murder One

Four threatening states of mind are considered to be the basis for a charge of Murder or Murder One: (1) The specific intent to kill another human being. This means the offender's intentional use of a deadly weapon against a vital part of the victim's body that results in death. (2) The specific intent of doing serious or fatal bodily harm to another person. (3) Willful and wanton life-threatening conduct upon another person. (4) The felony/murder rule, which means that the murder occurs during the commission of an inherently dangerous felony, such as robbery, rape, kidnapping, arson, or any other life-threatening felony.

The charge of Murder One requires both deliberation and premeditation, which demands that: (a) the offender had an intent to kill, (b) deliberation was present with the offender having a cool and calculating mind, (c) the murder was planned in advance of the commission of the act, with the offender having considered the ramification of the act and, despite the consideration, acted upon it.

"Murder One with Special Circumstances," wherein the killer has been charged with murder during a kidnapping or the killing of a law enforcement officer or has been laying in wait for his or her victim, is a charge that carries with it an automatic death penalty or life in prison without parole.

In either case—be it Murder One or Murder One with Special Circumstances—the prosecutor must prove that the victim is dead and that the victim's death was at the hands of the person accused of the murder. The death does not have to have occurred where the body is found, but the death of the victim must have occurred within a year and a day of the attack and be as a result of an attack by the accused.

Not all murders are intentional criminal attacks, although they are so classified. Many murders are the result of a dispute rather than a violent attack. In other words, an ongoing relationship can cause expectations and the failure to meet those expectations can produce anxiety, frustration, and anger, which then result in vengeance or retaliation. This brings up the question of who was responsible for the murder. Although the offender is the one who lives after the murder and a court and a jury will find the offender guilty of an evil doing, in a sense, the offender was provoked by the victim's inability to live up to the expectations of the relationship.

Murder in the Second Degree

This is the charge made against the offender when a murder has been committed without premeditation but in which the offender acted with specific intent or wanton and willful conduct to kill the victim.

Voluntary Manslaughter

Voluntary Manslaughter occurs when there are *mitigating circumstances*, such as the murder having been committed in the *heat of passion* and as a result of *reasonable provocation.*

But what is reasonable provocation? The general answer, not considering all the legal mumbo-jumbo, is that the offender must have had reasonable provocation, creating heated passion, which caused the offender to act without the intervention of any "reasonable" cooling-off period.

What is meant by provocation? Catching your mate in what appears to be an act of adultery, being involved in a physical altercation that escalates into murder, reacting to an assault or injury to someone close to you that results in a passionate response, thus causing provocation with the reaction being almost instantaneous.

Mitigating Circumstances

Many different extenuating circumstances might be considered to be mitigating circumstances. Three of the most common:

(1) *Diminished Capacity:* A mental disorder that is not considered insanity but that has legally psychologically affected the offender to such a degree that it affected the probability of malice, even though there was not necessarily specific intent to kill or wanton and willful conduct. Should you choose to use this as a defense in a story or screenplay, I suggest that you check the legality of this defense in the state in which your case is supposed to be tried.

(2) *Compulsion:* I strongly recommend that you check this area of mitigating circumstances with the laws of the state in which your story

takes place, finding what constitutes "compulsion" as a defense. I hasten to add that another psychological defense akin to compulsion is impulsion (uncontrollable impulsive behavior).

(3) *The Imperfect Right of Self-Defense* applies to someone who claims to have believed himself or herself to be in inherent danger but who was actually at fault for bringing about or acting upon an unreasonable yet honest belief that he or she was in danger.

MANSLAUGHTER

Although not legally considered murder or innocent homicide, manslaughter is the unlawful taking of a human life. What separates this charge from murder is that the charge does not require premeditation or malice aforethought.

There are two types of manslaughter—voluntary and involuntary. The difference between these two types involves whether or not the taking of human life was intended.

FEMALE MURDERERS

The most prominent characteristics of female murderers are that they are (1) Amoral, (2) Impulsive, (3) Jealous, (4) Insincere, (5) Self-Destructive, (6) Satanic, (7) Religiously Zealous, (8) Sociopathic.

Statistics reveal that the most common motives for female murderers are

- Profit
- Jealousy
- Revenge
- Sex
- Cult membership
- Tired of caring for a child or elderly person
- Inadequacy as a spouse or mother
- Under the influence of alcohol or drugs
- In need of money for drugs or alcohol
- Hormonal changes/premenstrual syndrome or post-partum depression.

CONTRACT KILLERS

Contract killers, otherwise known as professional hit men (although there are also some professional hit women), are cold blooded killers who have no feelings or compunctions as to whom they kill as long as they are paid to do the job. They are most often used by organized crime or street gangs, though hit men also are sometimes hired by non-professional criminals who are willing to pay to have someone killed.

"The Mark," as the selected victim is often referred to, is usually one who has been disloyal, has screwed up, or is a threat to the gang that issued the contract. Contracts have also been put out by those seeking to climb the ladder in some crime family or organization or to knock off the number-one man in an opposing family or gang.

Hit men have also been hired by civilians, people who are not professional criminals or a part of criminal society. The man or woman putting out the contract, for any number of reasons, will hire the pro because the non-pro cannot do the killing himself or herself or so that the non-pro can be miles away at the time of the killing, giving the non-pro a perfect alibi for the time the mark is killed.

The general method of execution is the small-caliber handgun, with one shot to the head. However, hit men have been known to use high-powered rifles, shotguns, pipe bombs, explosives placed under a car so that it explodes when the ignition is turned on, and, in some cases, letters or packages containing explosives that are activated when the letter or package is opened.

A hit can take place most anywhere: in a restaurant, a mall, a parking lot, or on the street, as in a drive-by shooting. Marks have also been "taken for a ride" to some remote place where the victim is shot once in the back of the head, and then the weapon discarded, usually in a river or lake where it is almost impossible for it to be found.

Organized Crime

When most people hear the term "organized crime," they automatically associate it with The Mafia or La Cosa Nostra when, in actuality, the term is generic. The term "organized crime" can be applied to any number of groups and gangs bound together as illicit business cartels to carry out an assortment of criminal ventures, much like a legitimate business conglomerate. The only difference between legitimate business and organized crime is the means by which they conduct their business ventures and, of course, the nature of those ventures—such as dealing in drugs, smuggling, gambling, racketeering, prostitution, and hundreds of other criminal activities. To this list, add murder or "whacking" or "wasting" or "taking down."

Organized-crime-related killings occur for a number of reasons: (1) a power struggle ensues among organized crime families, (2) someone inside a crime family or the organization has broken one of its rules or offended someone higher up in the organization, (3) to "enforce" or teach a lesson to someone in or out of the crime family. Most organized crime hits or murders are distinct in the sense that the victim is often killed in some ritualistic manner so that all are warned that this was done by an organized crime family.

Why would a criminal join or become a part of organized crime rather than work alone? For various reasons: Perhaps organized crime has issued a warning to that criminal to either become part of the syndicate *or else*, or becoming a part of a criminal combine brings the criminal more power and more operating capital. The larger the organization, the more benefits there are to be gained. It's no different than a legitimate business that offers its employees a number of benefits that they would find it hard to provide for themselves if they were self-employed. Organized crime offers its members legal aid, the assistance of corrupted politicians and law enforcement officers, and both financial and physical support. To put it plainly, organized crime has more fire power; and although your cut of the pie may be much smaller than if you were on your own, the size of the organized crime operation makes up for it in the long run. It should be noted, however, that different organizations have different operating procedures, and participation in the success and prosperity of the organization often depends on what rung of the ladder you are standing on. Soldiers in the Mafia have no piece of the action or any standing in the family until they become a "made" member or, as they say in the mob, "make their bones," which usually is accomplished by that Mafia soldier performing a hit.

The following is a list of the more prominent crime organizations:
The Italian/American Mafia
The Sicilian Mafia
The Russian Mafia
The Purple Gang
The Israeli Mafia
The Japanese and Korean Yakuza
The Chinese Triads
The Mexican Mafia (Eme)
Asian youth gangs
Vietnamese gangs
The Gypsy Mafia
Motorcycle gangs
Colombian cartels
Street gangs such as the Bloods, the Crips, the 18th-Street Gang, and a wide variety of neighborhood street gangs across the country.
Prison gangs
The Jamaican Posse
The National Crime Syndicate

And a wide variety of cults, terrorist organizations, and local and national crime organizations in every city and nation around the globe.

* * * * *

The Sicilian Mafia was formed in the late thirteenth century in Palermo, Italy. It originated as a secret society known as the Sicilian Vespers that sought to protect Sicilian citizens from the French Angevins invaders who were ruling over of Sicily. Successful in booting their oppressors out of their country and having grown in strength and power, in the fifteenth century they once again found themselves under foreign domination and were called upon to rid their country of the invading Bourbons, who were opposed by another secret society called the Camorra, which was composed primarily of criminals. The Vespers (now known as the Mafia) managed once again to rid their country of the foreign invaders, but not before the Mafia and the Camorra became entwined, the Mafia taking control of Sicily and the Camorra taking control of Naples.

Now more powerful than ever, the Mafia, no longer a patriotic and altruistic organization, turned to criminal activities that were extremely monetarily rewarding. By the turn of the nineteenth century, some of the members of the Sicilian Mafia and the Camorra decided to spread their wings and left the old country to establish themselves in the United States.

Until the late 1800s, most of the "organized" crimes on the east coast of the United States were committed by Irish gangs who ruled the ghettos until the arrival of the Italians and the Jews. But it was the Italians who succeeded first and foremost.

The Italian gangsters were originally known as The Black Hand and they rapidly became the plague of New York, especially in the Italian ghetto where they preyed first on their own immigrant people, causing local Italian businessmen to pay tribute to their society. The term Black Hand was born out of the fact that these Italian hoodlums' hands were usually black because the bodies of most of their murder victims were wrapped in black tar paper before they were dumped into the Hudson River or buried in unmarked graves. Eventually, as the Italian immigrants gained some affluence, they left their ghetto to the African Americans, Chinese, and Hispanics.

As the Mafia, also known as La Cosa Nostra (Our Thing), began to grow, it branched out like an octopus, its tentacles reaching out and taking hold of every conceivable criminal activity and vice, including gambling, prostitution, pornography, loan sharking, counterfeiting, drugs, smuggling, protection rackets, blackmail, record piracy, hijacking, arms sales, arson, insurance fraud, robbery, extortion, bootlegging, auto theft, and murder-for-hire.

But Meyer Lanskyand his brilliant criminal mind organized the Italians, the Jews, the Germans, the Irish, and many other criminal organizations of different nationalities to form the National Crime Syndicate, which then began invading hundreds of otherwise legitimate enterprises, such as trucking, restaurant supplies, unions, the apparel industry, the motion picture industry, laundries, and various businesses associated with the building industry, continuing to expand their criminal activities under the cover of legitimate businesses with which they could launder their money.

It has been often said that "they only kill their own." Not true—murder is still one of their major occupations, and they, like members of any of the criminal organizations listed above, will kill at the drop of a hat as long as it is profitable, gives them more power, rids them of competition, or merely throws fear into those they prey upon. Their number one business is Strictly Murder!

Little is known about the Mexican Mafia, "Eme" (the name it is known by), aside from the fact that many of its members are in jail serving long sentences for drug smuggling and murder. Practically all of Eme's operations are run by Mexican Mafia inmates, including the smuggling and dealing of drugs and, most assuredly, contracts for Mexican Mafia hit men on the outside.

⁎ ⁎ ⁎ ⁎ ⁎

Of the many organized crime mobs, the ones that are most active (and the ones that are most likely to be involved in violence and murder) are the American Mafia, the Colombian cartels, Asian gangs, the Yakuza, the Chinese Triads, the Mexican Mafia, the Russian Mafia (both in the U.S. and in Russia), and the numerous street gangs all across the country.

As for the American Mafia, it is now a far cry from its days of old and the "Mustache Petes." The American Mafia is heavily involved in "big business," its leaders well-educated and keeping a much lower profile than their predecessors.

The origin of the Chinese Triads is similar to that of the Sicilian Mafia—the Triads were secret patriotic organizations devoted to casting out the Europeans in what was known as the Boxer Rebellion. But they have long since abandoned any altruistic ventures in favor of more profitable criminal ventures. The Chinese Triads are the largest in both numbers and in income of all of those involved in organized crime, boasting a membership in Hong Kong alone of about 350,000, and their international income is rumored to be equivalent to all the American currency currently in circulation.

The Yakuza, which is the major organized crime element in Japan and Korea, is much like the American Mafia. They are referred to by the Japanese police as Boryokudan or "violent ones."

The most violent and murderous crime organizations are the Mexican Mafia, the Colombian cartels, Asian and American street gangs, and, notably, the Russian Mafia.

Although all of those organizations discussed above are heavily involved in murder, the Russian Mafia has the least regard for human life, and it has been rumored that their latest criminal activity is the kidnapping and murdering of innocent people, removing their vital organs, and selling body parts on the open market.

SUGGESTED READING

Double Cross: The Story of the Mobster Who Controlled America, Sam and Chuck Giancana, Warner Books, 1974.

The Mafia Encyclopedia, Carl Sifakis, Facts on File, 1987.

Men of Respect: A Social History of the Sicilian Mafia, Raimondo Catanzaro, Free Press, 1992.

The New Face of Organized Crime, G. J. Petrakis, Hunt Publications, 1992.
Organized Crime, Third Edition, H. Abadinsky, Nelson-Hall Publishers, 1990.

The following suggested material can be obtained from The National Institute of Justice, Clearing House Programs, Reference Department, Box 6000, Rockville, MD 20849-6000, 800-851-3420:

"Asian Gang Problems and Social Policy Solutions," *Gang Journal* V. 1, No. 4, 1993.
"New International Criminal and Asian Organized Crime," National Institute of Justice/National Justice Reference Service Paper Reproduction Sales, Box 6000, Department F, Rockville, MD 20850; DO Document -1993.
"Outlaw Motorcycle Gangs," *USA Overview*, National Institute of Justice/National Criminal Justice Reference Service Paper Reproduction Sales.
"Gang Violence and Organized Crime," National Institute of Justice, Dept. F, Rockville, MD 20850. (Also reprinted by National Youth Gang Information Center, Document Number J0028.)

Domestic Murders

Domestic murders all stem from one form of domestic violence or another, and that includes all violence within a family, between families, between adults and children who are related, and, of course, between lovers.

In spousal murders, the wife defendant is less likely to be convicted and, if convicted, less likely to receive a lengthy sentence than the husband defendant. The most common defenses for a woman are "victim provocation" and self-defense, which usually brings with them a lighter sentence should the wife be convicted.

Most wives who committed domestic murder used a gun or a knife in their assaults.

Sample cases:

(1) A husband constantly beats his wife. During a struggle, he picks up a knife and stabs her; she grabs the knife and stabs him, and he dies. She is arrested and claims self-defense. In court, the victim's family voices no objection to her plea and the woman goes free.

(2) A husband and wife have an altercation wherein she pulls out a gun and threatens to shoot him. He runs out of the house and gets into his car. She runs out, points gun at him, and he runs over her and is arrested the next day.

These are just two true cases. The first one gives you more of an idea for an ending. The second example has many possibilities. Using your own twists and turns, along with additional characters and relationships upon which to build characters, you might consider this as the opening or near opening of your filmscript. He could be an abuser, but then again, she could be an abuser, though it is usually difficult to accept such a plea because the man is usually the first one to be considered the aggressor in a marital murder. The husband's job (or that of a private investigator) is to prove that he killed her in self-defense. Not fair, you say, with women claiming to be man's equal. Unfortunately, the courts and law enforcement seldom see it that way.

PREMEDITATED SPOUSAL MURDERS

Premeditated murders among spouses are usually brought about for profit of some kind, either for insurance or such other financial gains as control of a business or the spousal victim's ongoing royalties or dividends.

Because the spousal offender is "usually" smart enough to know that a murder investigation is most likely to turn up the profit motive, the spousal offender will take great pains to make the murder appear to have been done by some unknown criminal by making the home or apartment appear to have been broken into and burglarized. This also calls for careful consideration as to the instrument of death. Unless the spousal offender is smart enough to know what poisons will not show up in a toxicology examination during an autopsy, the use of poisons is highly unlikely. The most probable weapon would be an unregistered gun that is then discarded so that it won't be found or a blunt instrument, preferably something in the home that the "burglar" picked up on the spur of the moment and then erased any trace of fingerprints.

Kids Who Kill & Killers of Kids

Be it some phenomena or just the crime-crazed world we live in now, more and more children are becoming both victims and perpetrators of murder. Here are some general statistics from the Department of Justice, Office of Juvenile Justice, about those who kill kids and kids who kill kids and some of the reasons why.

≤ Between the years 1980 and 1994, most children who were killed before the age of six were killed by a member of the family.
≤ Children under the age of six were usually beaten to death, while those over that age were usually killed by a firearm.
≤ Fifty percent more juvenile males where killed than juvenile females.
≤ Most older juveniles were killed by an acquaintance or a stranger.
≤ Ninety-three percent of black and white juvenile victims were killed by members of their own race.
≤ The increase in the number of juveniles murdered was highest among the youngest and the oldest juvenile groups.
≤ Trends reveal that acquaintances and strangers tend to use firearms when killing a juvenile.

Killers of Kids

The following are the most probable motives for the murder of a juvenile: (a) gang motivated, (b) abducted and murdered for sexual gratification (necrophilia or molestation), (c) thrill killing or enjoying the kill, (d) schoolyard arguments, (e) mental illness, (f) profit, (g) parental abuse, (h) a babysitter's impatience, (i) part of a murder/suicide committed by a family member, (j) robbery, (k) bullying, (l) revenge, (m) the result of punishment, (n) pedophile assault, (o) kidnapping.

Some unusual facts are associated with the murdering of juveniles, especially very young children: Most children are murdered by males; only twenty-five percent of all murders of juveniles are committed by females. Most males kill children for sexual gratification, while statistics reveal that a large percentage of juvenile murderers are females who commit these violent crimes purely for financial gain. Females also have a greater tendency to kill a small child because of annoyance or the inability to cope with the child or the child's behavior.

Kidnappings of juveniles that lead to murder are often due to (a) fear by the kidnapper that if the child was released, the child could identify the kidnapper, (b) the child was seriously hurt during a molestation by the kidnapper and died as a result of the molestation, (c) the kidnapper received sexual gratification by killing the child, (d) the kidnapping was purely for profit and the kidnapper never planned on returning the child once the kidnapper received the ransom.

Most kidnappings of juveniles involve the abductor snatching the child off the street, seeing a lost or wandering child in a mall and pretending to help the child find his or her parent, or luring their unsuspecting victims with a variety of promises or what a child would believe is a natural request. For example, an adult might offer a child the promise of ice cream or candy or a chance to play with a pet. Others might ask the child to help them locate a missing pet or find a particular location that the child is sure to know. Other lures include telling the child that his or her mother sent the adult to pick up the child at school, offering some valid reason why the parent was not able to be present. The longer the period of time the child is not returned or found, the more likely the child has been murdered and buried somewhere.

KIDS KILLING KIDS (AND ADULTS)

The following are the most probable motives for a juvenile committing murder: (a) gang related, (b) robbery, (c) racial or religious hatred,

(d) parental abuse, (e) protecting a family member, (f) drugs, (g) overbearing parents, (h) under the influence of drugs or alcohol, (i) carjacking, (j) forcible rape, (k) mental disorders such as impulsive/compulsive, attachment disorder, (l) parricide, (m) adolescent parricide, (n) stress.

There is little question that any single one or combination of the following four items are most accountable for juveniles committing criminal homicides:

(1) The amount of violence on television and in film that is seen by juveniles today and the way that fictional violence is committed. Years ago, in all areas of entertainment, evil was always punished in the end. Today, that is not necessarily the way many stories end. Juveniles have a strong desire to imitate, and seeing so much gratuitous violence and even the way murders are committed gives many of today's youth a sick outlook on life. Many very young juveniles have little if any idea what the repercussions are to the taking of another life. Those who are abused see a means of striking back or releasing their aggression on someone else. Others believe that killing is a means to an end, a way of survival on our mean streets. Still others see so much violence around them that life itself has no value.

(2) We have taken the white hat off the hero's head and put the black hat on the hero as well as the bad guy. In other words, we have so impugned and maligned the image of the police and law enforcement today that children have little if any respect for law and order. They not only see this on television shows and in motion pictures but in the news, where the media delights in stories about bad or rogue cops. Many of their parents who were baby boomers looked upon police and law enforcement as "pigs," and with their parents not having any respect for law enforcement, the children also fail to show any respect for law enforcement. It's unfortunate, but most young people today do not trust the police.

(3) Although today's economy appears to require both parents to be employed, the absence of at least one parent at home has produced a generation of latchkey kids who more often than not wind up on the street, unsupervised, and thus being drawn to neighborhood gangs that become their "family" or getting into mischief on their own.

(4) Probably the single most important reason for kids killing kids and for kids killing adults today is the ease with which juveniles can buy or come into possession of guns and drugs, which are readily available to juveniles not only on the street but right in the schoolyard. The number of guns brought onto school grounds and into classrooms is almost unfathomable today. What else can we expect but strictly murder!

Statistics reveal that three out of every five people who committed a violent crime against children under the age of twelve are adults. Statistics also reveal that young offenders are more likely to commit violent crimes against victims their own age and that juveniles are more likely to commit violent crimes in groups rather than by themselves.

SUGGESTED READING

"Juveniles Processed in Criminal Court and Case Dispositions," General Accounting Office, Washington, DC.

Juvenile Offenders and Victims: A National Report, U.S. Department of Justice, Office of Juvenile Justice and Delinquency Prevention, Washington, DC 20531.

1996 Update on Violence: Juvenile Offenders and Victims, U.S. Department of Justice, Office of Juvenile Justice, Washington, DC 20531.

Why Kids Kill Parents: Child Abuse and Adolescent Homicide, Ohio State University Press.

Serial Killers

Serial killers are not new nor unique. They have existed for centuries in both fact and fiction, from Dracula to Jack the Ripper to Ted Bundy to Jeffrey Dahmer and the Night Stalker, Richard Ramirez.

Today, we are especially aware of their existence because of the media frenzy that surrounds them when they strike. Serial killers like The Green River Strangler have become cause célèbres. And law enforcement officials guesstimate that somewhere between 2,000 and 5,000 serial killers are roaming our streets. A very frightening thought.

Serial killers should not be confused with mass murderers like Richard Speck or the Texas Tower killer, Charles Whitman, who stood atop a university tower and shot at everyone in sight, killing more than twenty innocent people.

Serial killers are unique unto themselves, willing and capable of living out and fulfilling their fantasies. Statistically, most serial killers are males between the ages of twenty-five and thirty-four. Most are indiscriminate, felony murderers.

‣ ‣ ‣ ‣ ‣

Uniform crime reports that are sent to VICAP are broken down into numeric codes that categorize the type of homicide, such as 508.01, meaning a criminal enterprise homicide, while another numeric code might refer to group-excitement homicides or indiscriminate homicides. In the case of a serial killer, the VICAP might read something like "H. M. N.Y.C. 38-97 508.04," which would translate to "Homicide, Male, New York City, the 38-97 meaning it was the 38th killing in that city in 1997. The numeric code that follows indicates that the killing was of an indiscriminate nature and apparently not planned in advance with any specific victim in mind. A further search of VICAP could reveal a pattern that indicates that ten of those killings might easily have been the work of one person.

In many instances, those killed in an indiscriminate manner probably did not know their killer, and the killing was not motivated by any sexual act or any desire for personal gain, but rather was motivated by some emotional conflict or some socially or personally aggravated condition in the mind of the serial killer.

Serial killers are not born. They are made by certain conditions that bring about the desire to kill, usually because of parental abuse the killer suffered as a child. Naturally, not all abused children become serial killers. It takes a certain disposition and psychological makeup for a child to develop into a serial killer.

Generally, serial killers come from minimum-wage-earning families and lower-middle-class homes. More often than not, they were abused as children or came from broken homes. Their parents may have been drug addicts, alcoholics, religious fanatics, or just plain abusers. Most serial killers will seek out their victims from the upper class, and usually seek out female victims upon whom they can vent their hostility, aggression, and power/control. And, usually, they have no remorse or feelings of guilt for the crimes they commit.

Although there are many psychologically defined types of serial killers, here are the basic four:

(1) The Visionary, who is really quite insane. Other types often know the nature of the acts they perform, but the Visionary often hallucinates, hears voices, and sees visions that order him to kill. He believes himself to be controlled by God, the Devil, or other demons.

(2) The Mission-Oriented serial killer is out of control. He needs to dominate and control others, does not consider his conduct to be asocial, and basically uses his killings as a means of achieving irrational goals against society, e.g., seeking to rid the world of prostitutes, bums, the poor, the ill, etc.

(3) The Hedonistic serial killer kills for the pure pleasure of killing.

He usually experiences a "rush" during the act of killing and following a sexual attack. This one is the most transient, often moving from place to place.

(4) The Power Control killer gains his gratification from exercising complete control over his victim. Although sex sometimes is involved, the superiority over his victim is more important than his sexual gratification.

It should be noted that few serial killers "just commit murders" and leave it at that. There are those who suffer from what is classified as erotomania; they commit fantasy killings brought about by the serial killer's fusion of identities. Many, in addition to their fantasy, have some sort of fetish or need to do something to the remains of their victims. This ranges from having sex with their victims (after death) to dismembering them and, often, saving many of the body parts and, on occasion, even cannibalizing their victims, often with the desire to attain celebrity status. These killers are called "collectors."

Another category is that of the Extremist, whose mental state is characterized by an overpowering religious or political belief.

Some serial killers mentally kill the same individual over and over again in their own minds, never satisfied that the victim is actually dead. These killers have been known to make up their victims to resemble someone else they have known—often a parent or former lover—whom they believe they are killing over and over again.

Although typology differs from one serial killer to another, generally, serial killers are selfish, intelligent with superficial charm, and often use some sort of ruse to gain control over their victim. Serial killers, generally ambitious in seeking social standing, have often experienced aggression, frustration, and abuse and feel emasculated.

When dealing with serial killers, it is important to note that most of them fall into two basic categories: the *organized* serial killer and the *disorganized* serial killer.

The organized one is often highly intelligent, sexually and socially competent, and both ingratiating and mobile. He can easily be recognized as "organized" because his behavior indicates careful planning before an attack on a stranger. Once he selects his victims and gains the upper hand, he will personalize his victims, requiring them to be totally submissive. Control is essential because the organized killer is somewhat of a control freak. He will toy with his victims, often using restraints, and, after killing them, will make sure he leaves no evidence behind.

The disorganized killer is just the opposite of his counterpart. He has little patience, will attack spontaneously and usually with great violence. He does not have the intelligence that the organized killer has, is impersonal, and seldom converses with or bothers to toy with his victims. He invariably has sex with his victims before and after he has killed them and is often careless when it comes to leaving evidence behind.

You must have noticed that I have primarily referred to serial killers as masculine. My reason for this is that most serial killers are male. But let's not completely overlook:

THE FEMALE SERIAL KILLER

Female serial killers are intelligent and usually older than their male counterparts by three to five years. The majority of female serial killers are white and upper-middle class. Statistically, they are nurses, housekeepers, homemakers, waitresses, or college students.

The victims of female serial killers range from patients entrusted to their care, pick-ups, hitchhikers, total strangers, roomers, tenants, children, the elderly, a series of husbands, in-laws, and a series of lovers or boyfriends.

Their weapon of preference, in fifty percent of the cases, is poison; in the remaining fifty percent of the cases, female serial killers do their killing by shooting, bludgeoning, stabbing, suffocating, neglecting, and drowning.

Note: The FBI Psychological Evaluation Section in Quantico, Virginia, compiles many of the available statistics on serial killers, and a retired agent, John Douglas, wrote a book, *Manhunter*, that may answer some of your questions. Other excellent books on the subject include *Serial Killers* by Joel Norris; *Sexual Homicide: Patterns and Motives* by R. K. Ressler, A.W. Burgess, and J.E. Douglas (Lexington Books, 1988); *The Age of Sex Crime* by Jane Caputi (Bowling Green State University Press, 1987); and *The Serial Killers* (Carol Publishing Group, 1991).

Sex & Murder

Sex and murder often go hand in hand. Murders tied to sex may be the result of rape, gang rape, spousal rape, incest, homosexual sex, sexual misconduct by a doctor, assault on a child or infant, sexual slavery, prostitution, or, in one of the most unusual cases of sexual murder, "abortional homicide," where an irate ex-husband brutally assaulted his pregnant ex-wife and caused the death of her unborn child.

Most sex-related murders are the result of an expression of power and could be considered a result of the Expressive Homicide Syndrome, especially if the sexual act is committed out of anger or sadism. There are cases, however, where the Instrumental Syndrome would come into play, in which event the perpetrator looked upon his sexual conquest as his "property" and killed because of that fixation.

The Act of Terrorism: Preface

By Dr. Stephen Sloan

Dr. Stephen Sloan is a Professor of Political Science at the University of Oklahoma, where he has been a member of the faculty since 1966. He received his B.A. from Washington Square College of New York University and his M.A. and Ph.D. from the Graduate School of Arts and Sciences, New York University. He has been a Fulbright Professor at Tribhuvan University, Kathmandu, Nepal; Senior Research Fellow at the Center for Aerospace Doctrine Research and Education, Air University, Maxwell AFB, Montgomery, Alabama (GM-15 equivalent 1984-86); a Senior Associate at Booze, Allen & Hamilton, Inc.; Head of Counter Terrorism for Intelligence Systems Practice, Washington, D.C.; and has served as a contributor to the Vice President's Task Force on Combating Terrorism.

First I wish to make it clear that I have been concerned over the years that both print and electronic media have, in too many cases, engaged in stereotyping terrorist behaviors. These stereotypes are often quite superficial and do not deal with the dynamics and underlying courses that lead individuals and groups to engage in terrorist acts. As such, authors and writers then unintentionally glamorize the acts of terrorism by playing into the stereotypes of those who engage in violence. One should avoid such stereotypes and develop a well-grounded knowledge of terrorism and strategies, becoming sensitive to the dynamics of terrorism and attempting to ascertain the complex environment of today's and the future's terrorist groups.

Those who engage in murder as an aspect of terrorism often are involved in what is called purposeful violence. That is, they do not engage in an act based on the heat of violence as, for example, seen in domestic-violence disputes. In a sense, their resort to murder has a degree of "rationality" in that it is a planned act. Obviously, there may be more deeply embedded psychological reasons why people engage in carnage and terrorism that are based on more deeply held and often irrational beliefs. However, at least on the surface and in regard to many acts, the murder is a purposeful one.

In many instances, the violence that does take place in the form of murder is not simply directed at an individual; indeed, the individual may be, unfortunately, nothing more than a "walking symbol." In the case of warfare, there may be the intentional view that the victim can be dehumanized and, therefore, it is easier to kill "him" or "her." In this sense, a police officer, a multi-national executive, a senior political leader, etc., may be the subject of assassination because of what they symbolize. As I note in some of my exercises, when the gun is pointed at the individual's head, the perpetrator often says, "Don't take this personally—I am engaging in violence for what you stand for." I specifically recall an incident where West German terrorists justified the murder of a West German pilot by saying that the pilot was essentially "dealing with a German technocratic mind." Hence, the dehumanization of the victim.

In regard to an act of murder as an aspect of terrorism, the ultimate target may not, ironically, be the immediate victim but the broader audience. In essence, the terrorist may kill an individual or individuals as a means of intimidating a broader audience. Analytically speaking, this means that while, outwardly, the victim would appear to be the primary target, in reality, he, she, or they would be the secondary target because the ultimate target is the government, the corporation, or the broader audience that the terrorist, through the murderous act, wants to intimidate.

The resort to murder by the terrorist often is justified, if not motivated, by political reasoning. The resort to murder is legitimized as if it were a valid "act of war" against the symbols of a "repressive regime."

Finally, I must again note that the ultimate motivation for an act of murder as an act of terrorism, however defined in terms of political justification, is nothing more than an act of irrationality. Terrorism, as in the case of a wide variety of other forms of violence, has its own dynamics, and the underlying, or indeed the precipitating courses of that violence, may ultimately have nothing to do with why the act was committed. For example, after the fact, an individual with a terrorist organization may justify his or her actions on the basis of fighting for his or her cause, but that cause may not be related to the dynamics of a strife when one side wants to get even with another side. In that sense, terrorism is a form of action and reaction, violence and murder in a form of revenge.

TERRORISM

Before getting down to the nitty-grittiness of this chapter, we must first define the word "terrorism"—it has a multiplicity of commonly assumed meanings, although terrorism ultimately ends in murder, either of an individual or a group of people.

In its essence, terrorism is a premeditated act of violence that is racially, religiously, or politically motivated, with the violent action taken primarily against non-combatant people or individuals by subnational groups or clandestine organizations whose purpose is to influence, antagonize, or intimidate a political party, a government, or a nation as to the terrorist group or organization's cause. (Note: Not all acts or terrorism are against non-combatants as in the case of the terrorist attack on American military serving as peacemakers in Lebanon. Terrorists are also a part of guerrilla warfare, commando raids, and insurgency and counter-insurgency warfare.)

Unfortunately, as Dr. Sloan indicates in his Preface, the print, electronic, and film media all too often misrepresent terrorists as gross stereotypes, making them appear as unshaven, unkempt, ignorant, and impatient Arabs bent on killing anybody and everybody who gets in their way when, in truth, most terrorists are clever, intelligent, and well-trained individuals. Many of today's terrorists are well-educated, their radical beliefs beginning during protest rallies in their college years. Others begin as high-school dropouts who, for a myriad of reasons, became disillusioned with government or society and, like some who have joined cults or militia groups, plan to commit terrorist acts in defiance or to attempt one day to overthrow government. Most are dedicated to their causes, many are fanatical and have complete disregard for the lives they take as long as it serves their cause.

Terrorism is not necessarily an act of violence committed by an individual or group from a foreign county. The Oklahoma bombing, which not only took down the Federal building but killed hundreds of innocent men, women, and children, was committed by American citizens as an act of defiance against their own government. Terrorism is a very complex term, and to further understand terrorism's goals, objectives, and operations, we must attempt to understand the mind of the terrorist.

Most of the time, we think of a terrorist as a man. It's true. Most terrorists have, in the past, been males. However, the world has changed, and more and more women and even small children now play a large part in acts of terrorism. We found this to be true in the Vietnam War and, in the past fifty years, in the Middle East, the Far East, and Africa.

• • • • •

We can trace acts of terrorism back to the American Revolution (the British considered The Boston Tea Party an act of terrorism), the Comanche and Apache tribes in their war against the United States Government, both the North and the South in our own Civil War, the Nazi youth groups and the Gestapo in Nazi Germany, and many of the party members in Communist Russia. Terrorism does not belong to any one country, race, religion, or people. Terrorism, in essence, is extremism and can be found anywhere extremists with a cause exist.

It is not easy to become a terrorist. To become one, the individual must be willing to take high risks, even to the extent of sacrificing his or her life for the cause of a particular group. A terrorist must believe with his or her heart and soul that all who oppose the aims and goals of the movement are evil and that evil must be taught a lesson and punished if not done away with altogether.

A terrorist must be committed and single-minded as to his or her cause, and cannot be swayed into believing anything he or she does is wrong or immoral. To the terrorist, whatever he or she does is justified.

A terrorist must be totally devoted not only to his or her cause but also to his or her leader and be willing to follow that leader blindly and without question.

A terrorist must be completely without feelings, must be cold and indifferent to human life. Terrorists must have no remorse for whatever act of violence they have committed. To restate their commitment, all who oppose them are "the enemy."

Terrorist groups are akin to cults, and their leaders seek cult-member types to enlist in their cause, preferably those who are willing to surrender their personal possessions and devote themselves only to the goals of the organization.

Among the people most likely to join these entities are those who (a) have grievances that can be exploited, (b) feel unjustly deprived by the society they have been living in, (c) are idealists, (d) seek to enhance their position of power in their country or in the world, (e) willingly surrender their own personal identities in favor of a leader and an organization that expresses the ideology or cause to which they wish to dedicate themselves, (f) for a lack of a sense of belonging, become a member of cult or organization, which in turn they accept as their family or brotherhood, (g) seek immortality by becoming a martyr for a cause, (h) wish to feel invincible and superior to others outside their own organization, (i) can be brainwashed into believing in a terrorist cause.

TERRORISM: Q & A

Q: What are the most prominent terrorist organizations, aside from the much-publicized PLO?
A: There are estimated to be more than 400 terrorists organizations worldwide. The following are just a few of those that have become more prominent because of the media: the IRA, the Japanese Red Army, the Italian Red Brigade, the KKK, Neo-Nazis, Skinheads, Hezbollah, the former Baader-Meinhof gang (now known as the Red Army Fraction), and the Tupac Amaru Revolutionary Movement (MRTA), which recently took over the Japanese Embassy in Peru and held hundreds of dignitaries from all over the world hostage.

Q: Can you tell me anything about the organization known as the Red Army Fraction? When were they formed and what are their goals?
A: They are an anarchistic leftist group that formed around 1972 and has been involved in numerous attacks on the West German government, including bombings, hostage taking, assassinations, and other international operations.

Q: Are there links between various terrorist organizations around the world?
A: Occasionally they will communicate or assist one another if it is to their mutual benefit; however, most of them maintain strict security and keep to themselves. Terrorist organizations in the U.S. have more of a tendency to link with other group within the U.S., as opposed to international organizations.

Q: In the event there was a terrorist nuclear threat, who would be lead-

ing the investigation?
A: Obviously the FBI, but probably the most important agency would be NEST (Nuclear Emergency Search Teams), who would investigate if the threat was real.

Q: What can you tell me about the Baader-Meinhof Gang?
A: The Baader-Meinhof Gang was organized by Andreas Baader and Uhlrike Meinhof sometime around 1968. The organization was disbanded after Baader and Meinhof were arrested and committed suicide in or about 1972. Those who were left became part of the Red Army Fraction.

Q: What is the difference between the front and the combat cell?
A: The front is the organization that controls a number of "cells" that perform a variety of activities which help make the organization function, such as lobbying various governments and getting financial and sympathetic support from governments, organizations, industrialists and individuals who sympathize with their cause. A "combat cell" is that part of the front that is responsible for carrying out acts of terrorism on behalf of the front.

Q: What are the primary targets of terrorists: taking hostages, blowing up military installations, killing innocent civilians?
A: Usually, hostage-taking has a two-pronged purpose. One is to use the hostages as a bargaining tool, possibly to get other imprisoned terrorists freed from prison, but also to gain a great deal of media attention and coverage. The purpose of killing innocent civilians is to frighten and intimidate the civilian population in the hope that they will bear down on their government to meet the terrorists' demands. Terrorists adhere to Sun Szu's adage: "Kill one person, frighten a thousand."

Terrorist cells seldom target military installations. Although terrorists have attacked military installations on occasion, as they did to the U.S. military base in Lebanon, in most scenarios, military installations are of little value in the war that terrorists wage. Terrorists prefer attacking an embassy for symbolic reasons.

Q: It seems to me that although the Catholic Church appears to oppose acts of terrorism, they also have condoned some terrorist acts. How can they go both ways?
A: It depends on whether the Catholic Church is subscribing to the doctrine of "Liberation Theology," which justifies certain acts of terrorism as acts of liberation against repressive regimes.

Q: What do you advise (morally) when I, as a writer, come up with a very violent terrorist concept for a film I am writing, knowing full well that I may be putting an idea into someone's head when they see the film?
A: My practical answer is that you are not the only writer out there who may have come up with your idea or a very similar one. I understand your concern, but many films and stories containing violent terrorist acts have been written by former military men or law enforcement officers who went ahead and openly displayed their ideas regardless of such concerns as yours. My only suggestion is to discuss your idea with a law enforcement agency so they can be prepared should some organization or nut out there decide to actually act on your ideas.

SUGGESTED READING

Historical History of Terrorism, Sean Anderson and Stephen Sloan, Scarecrow Press.
The Morality of Terrorism: Religious and Secular Justification, David C. Rapoport and Yonah Alexander.
Baader-Meinhof Complex, Stefan Aust.
Blood and Rage: The Story of the Japanese Red Army, William Farrell, Lexington Books, 1990.

There are several extensive bibliographies on international terrorism, from the early 1970s to the present. Check your libraries for authors Edward F. Mickolus, Guy D. Boston, and M.C. Bassiouni. You also might contact the Washington State University library, which has Terrorist Group Profiles, and the *Ohio University Intelligence*

Sourcebook, which offers an in-depth history of terrorist groups. Last, but not least, any college library designated as a Federal Depository often has an excellent selection of background material on terrorism, as does the Superintendent of Documents in Washington, D.C. Interpol is another source that collects data on terrorism throughout the world.

Cults That Kill: Preface

By Dr. Hannah Evans

> "Going around hypnotized all the time, what brains he had—not a whole lot to start with, she says—had become completely scrambled. His success in flimflamming his followers had gone to his head. He thought he could do anything. He had dreams, she says, of the entire world deluded into belief in his divinity: he didn't see that that would be any—or much—more difficult than fooling the handful he had fooled. She thinks he actually had insane notions of his own divinity. I don't go that far. I think he knew well enough that he wasn't divine but thought he could kid the rest of the world. These details don't make much difference; the thing is that he was a nut who saw no limit to his power."
>
> —Dashiell Hammett, *The Dain Curse*, 1928

Hammett could have been describing Koresh, Manson, perhaps Jones. What it comes down to is an ego trip by a charismatic figure with a vision and vulnerable followers. The notion of the vision is irrelevant when considering the makeup of the cult leader.

Cults & Sects

First, we must separate sects from cults. Too often, people tend to confuse one with the other. A sect requires no leader and thus can last much longer than a cult that depends greatly on its leader—and when the leader dies, as in the case of The People's Temple, the cult dies with him or her, as the case may be. Opus Dei, on the other hand, best fits the concept of a sect—it lasted more than a hundred years and had no charismatic leader. We should not consider Satanism as a cult either: Although we might consider The Prince of Darkness, Auld Horne, Lucifer, Old Nick, Mephistopheles, Beelzebub, or whatever name the followers of Satan refer to him as a charismatic leader, Satanism is actually defined as worshipping the Christian Lord of Hell and all that is non-Christian. As such, it is considered today to be a legally recognized religion. This, of course, is not meant to imply that there is no relationship between Satanism and crime and murder. However, those studying Satanic organizations claim that The Church of Satan and the Temple of Set are devoid of any criminal activity. (This claim does not exclude a number of Satanic cults that have specific leaders who are bent on committing violent sex crimes, human sacrifices, and cold-blooded murder, the worst of which, so far, has been the Manson Family.)

The Occult Versus the Cult

Writers often confuse the occult and those who deal in witchcraft and other neo-pagan beliefs with murderers. Although it may make for a good story, it is more dramatic license than it is truth—violence is seldom employed by most followers of the occult. Those involved in witchcraft or in various aspects of parapsychology or metaphysics are mostly non-violent individuals who stress freedom, preach no harm to anyone, and, in practically all cases, prohibit human sacrifice.

Law enforcement agencies involved in cult-related murders and ritualistic sexual abuses of children or adults that result in murder often reveal that the perpetrators belong to some Christian fundamentalist group, such as those involved in the Waco, Jonestown, and Mormon murders as opposed to those who are associated with a satanic coven.

Not to be overlooked in those cults involved in violence and criminal homicide are members of the KKK, white supremacists, the Aryan Nation, and the Neo-Nazis, to name just a few of the non-religious or more militaristic organizations responsible for cold-blooded murders. Add to this list dozens of armed camps, militias, and communes made up of American citizens much like the one in Waco, Texas, who, despite the outcome in Waco, continue to prepare for armed conflict with our society and our government. Then there is The Identity Movement Church and its militaristic wing that bears the title "The Covenant, the Sword and the Arms of the Lord." The CSA, as it is often called, has endorsed any and all acts of terrorism and murder against blacks and other non-whites, Jews, and non-Christians in a war they now violently wage against innocent men, women, and children and the government of the United States. As I wrote earlier in the chapter on Terrorism, do not visualize all terrorist and political, racial, and religious murderers as ignorant Arabs with five o'clock shadows. Our country already has too many people who embrace violence to further their irrational beliefs.

VICTIMS

Everyone is a potential victim today because the value of human life appears to have diminished faster than profits in the stock market.

During the past few years, the trend in murder has changed drastically for the young people in this country. From 1965 to 1985, the average age for becoming a murderer or a victim of murder was between eighteen and twenty-four. Since then it has dropped to the almost inconceivable range of ten to fourteen. This change is primarily attributed to drugs and street gangs and the growing use of guns by juveniles. The risk of victimization for young people increased greatly from the late 1980s to the mid 1990s—one hundred fifty percent for ages five to twelve and ten to fourteen and ninety-five percent for ages fifteen to nineteen. The ever-increasing trend of juveniles becoming offenders is matched by the ever-increasing trend of juveniles becoming victims.

Statistics seem to conclude that the older you get, the odds of you becoming a murder victim decrease greatly. Naturally, all of these statistics depend largely on what in police parlance has become known as Homicide Syndromes.

Homicide Syndromes fall into a variety of categories, which include Expressive and Instrumental, lethal sibling offenses, and Homicide/Violence, which combines any two or all three of the previously mentioned syndromes.

In Instrumental violence, the perpetrator's primary motive is to acquire money or property. Instrumental violence includes violence committed during robbery, burglary, arson for profit, drug deals, and contract killings. The Instrumental Syndrome also includes rape of either sex and murder brought about by street gangs defending their turf, recruiting, setting examples, and seeking revenge against other gangs or gang members.

In the Expressive Syndrome, the motive is the violence itself. Expressive violence syndrome can be broken down to include violence between spouses, ex-spouses, boyfriends and girlfriends, ex-boyfriends and ex-girlfriends, and homosexual domestic violence. Other Expressive Syndromes include child abuse by a parent or caretaker; confrontations between relatives; violence erupting between neighbors, friends, and co-workers, violence as part of a barroom brawl with a stranger; age-related and sex-related abuse; hate crimes; and random shootings.

Not included in either of these syndromes are murder/suicides and mercy killings, where passion, depression, or concern is the motive.

EXAMINING AND IDENTIFYING THE VICTIM

A well-trained investigator will never rely completely on visual identification, even the identification of the victim by a supposed friend, relative, or neighbor of the victim, or on written documents, driver's licenses, or personal articles.

Although the identification based on such evidence may be valid, the investigator will still check the victim's fingerprints, dental charts, medical records, and body marks (such as surgical scars, former wounds, and tattoos). The investigator will also thoroughly check the condition of the victim's clothing—whether it is old, new, disheveled, cut, ripped, unfastened, torn, partially removed; where and when the clothing was purchased and cleaned; and any foreign substances that may have attached themselves to the victim's clothing, such as dust, food stains, dog or cat hairs, human hairs, and fibers from other clothing, rugs, and furniture. Additionally, the investigator will search for and check any watch or jewelry that the victim may be wearing or that the victim was known to wear but is found to be missing.

Most important is that the investigator have the Medical Examiner determine as precisely as possible the time when death occurred. This is done through brain, rectal, and liver temperatures, the position of the victim's body when the attack and/or death occurred, and a consideration of control factors, such as climatic conditions, lividity, rigor mortis, liver mortis, and the victim's state of putrefaction. The medical examiner's determination of the time of death will not only fix the time of the murder but also help determine whether the victim was killed in the location and position he or she was found in or had been moved from one position to another or one location to another.

The investigator should learn as quickly as possible the victim's

- former mental state
- financial condition (including wills, insurance policies, bank accounts)
- addictions, if any
- special habits or vices
- sexual preferences
- recent sexual encounters
- former police records
- association with known criminals
- changes in marital status
- changes in relationships
- relationships with friends and business acquaintances
- recent firing of employees
- former wounds (and how obtained)
- membership in any secret societies or cults

HOMICIDE PHOTOGRAPHS

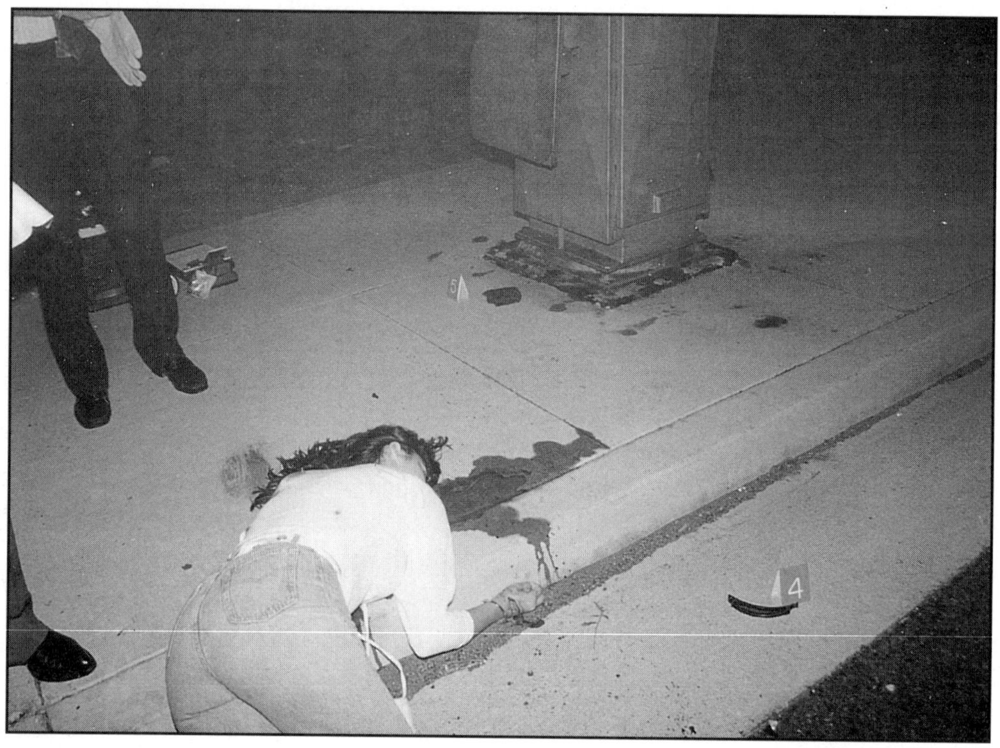

Crime scene. Note criminalist from CSU (Crime Scene Unit) putting on gloves before touching anything.

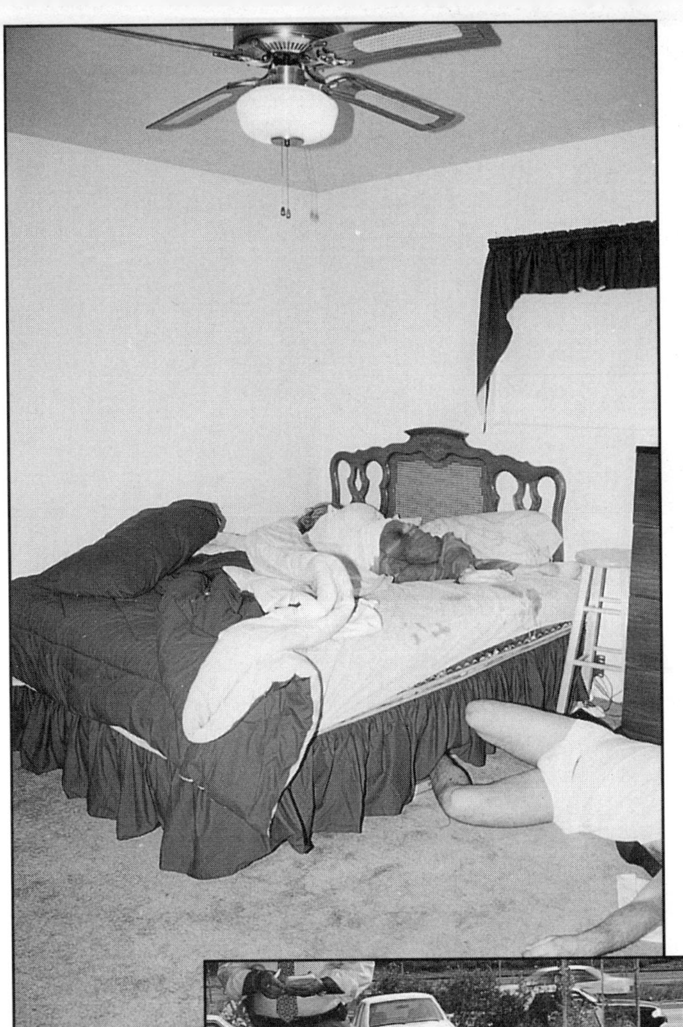

Another crime scene. One body on bed and one on the floor.

Crime scene. Numbers show position of shells fired from weapon.

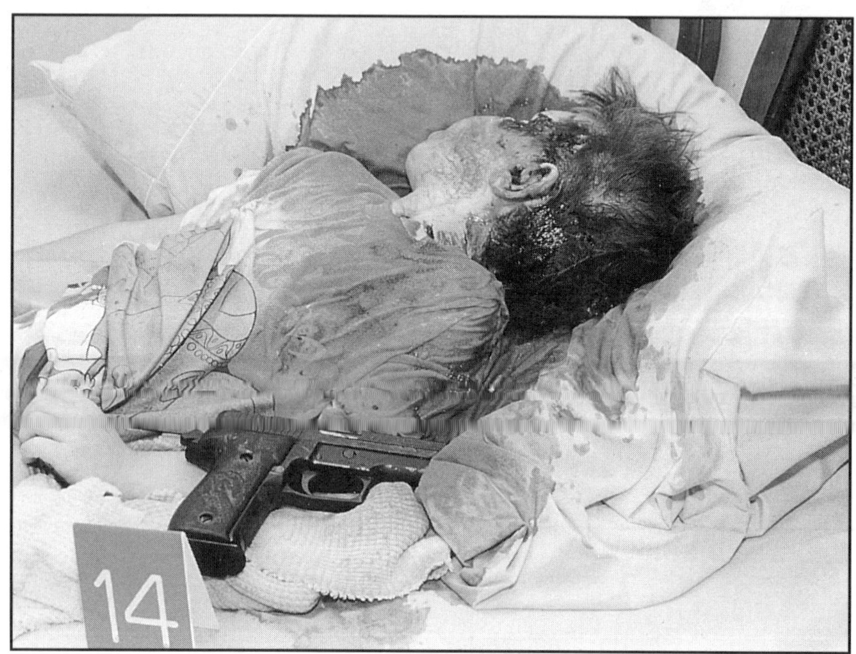

Body of victim who has "bled out" due to gunshot wounds.

Human remains that have decayed through exposure to natural elements.

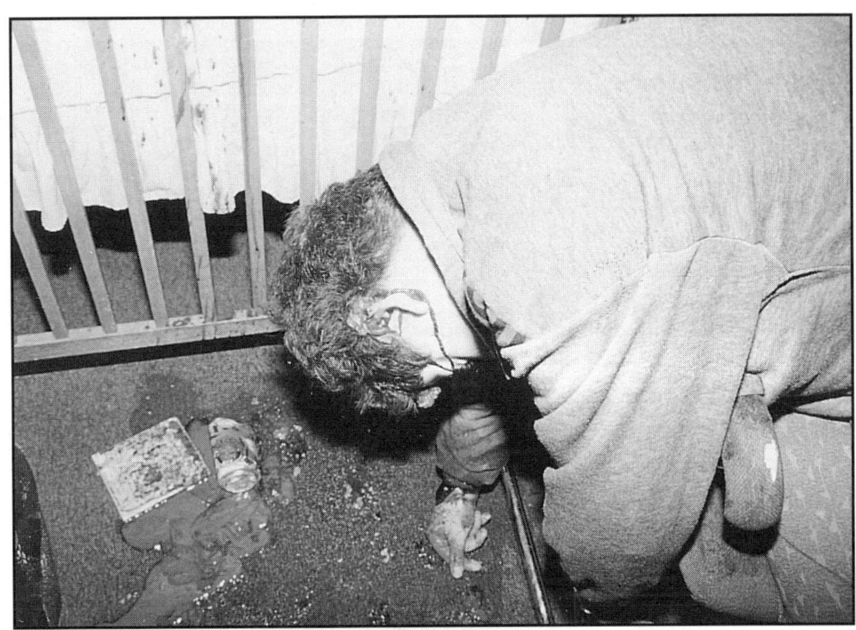

Left side of victim's neck and head, slashed and stabbed.

This is a "staged" scene. Staging, or altering the scene, is generally done by a suspect after the crime to lead the authorities in a false direction. Staging may also occur when the body is found by a close friend or relative, to cover a body and therefore lend some dignity to the deceased.

The back of a victim showing post-mortem lividity. This is where the blood sinks to the lowest portion of the body due to the forces of gravity. Generally occurs one to two hours after death. Note the "blanched" area. This victim has been turned over sometime *after* death. Lividity could be important in determining whether or not a victim has been moved or "dumped."

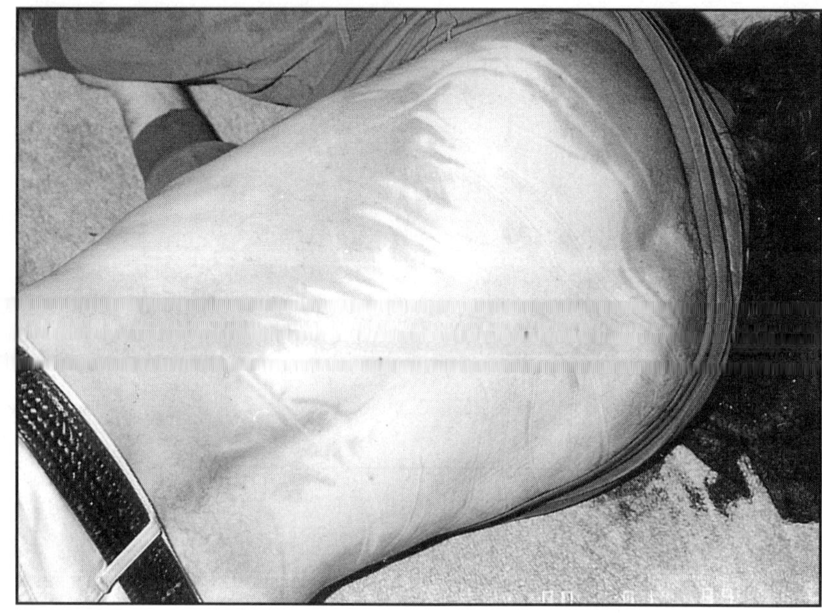

Murder Weapons & the Means to Murder

Listing all of the weapons and devices that have been used to take human life would literally be impossible. However, I will attempt to list as many as I can.

Strangling and Hanging

- Rope
- Wire
- Belt
- Clothing
- Sheet
- Hands
- Towel
- Choke collar
- Cable
- Electric cord
- Metal chain

Shooting

- Revolver
- Automatic
- Semi-automatic
- Shotgun
- Double-barreled shotgun

- Sawed-off shotgun
- Rifle

ASPHYXIATION

- Pillow
- Plastic bag
- Drowned by holding head under water
- Choking
- Buried alive

STABBING, CUTTING, HACKING

- Knife
- Axe
- Hatchet
- Saw
- Chainsaw
- Machete
- Scalpel
- Scissors
- Nail file
- Straight razor
- Blade
- Fork
- Spear
- Pointed pole
- Pitchfork
- Ice pick
- Screwdriver
- Hypodermic needle

BLUNT TRAUMA

- Baseball bat

- Two-by-four
- Hammer
- Brass knuckles
- Lamp
- Stone
- Lead pipe

Other Weapons and Means

- Poison
- Fire
- Acid
- Explosive
- Electric shock
- Vehicle
- Poisonous snake
- Poisonous gas
- Poisonous insect
- Vicious animal
- Starvation
- Falls from high places
- Bad drugs
- Lethal injection
- Exposure to lethal disease

A Note to Writers

There is no one way to take the life of another human being. It all depends on the frame of mind of the murderer prior to and when committing a murder, and the time and place chosen to commit the murder.

The killer may just walk into a room and start firing or come up behind the victim and cut the victim's throat. Then there's always stabbing, poisoning, strangling, or suffocating. Quite ordinary. There's no pizzazz.

How about burning, decapitating, chopping into little pieces, drowning or maybe feeding to the fish, dropping from an airplane, burying alive or in quicksand, staking to an anthill, or leaving the victim in alligator-infested swamps? Hanging? Too simple. Why not drop the victim inside a volcano or into an active volcano's molten lava? That's a hot one.

How about the zoo? Your victim could be stomped by an elephant or chewed up by lions or tigers. Gorillas or boa constrictors might hug him or her to death or a python might swallow your victim whole.

You could burn your victim up in a nice cozy fire or impale him or her. You could shock your victim to death or scare your victim to death by heart attack. Oh, I'm sure you'll think of something.

What is important to the writer is finding something unique—something that will terrify the viewer or the reader and cause the investigators problems in their discovery of the body or the motive or the type of killer they are after. However, should you wish to go the old-fashioned way—shooting the victim—here's the sequence of the shooting:

When a firearm is fired, it emits a cloud of gas from the barrel followed by a flame that appears for a brief instant. The bullet (the projectile), once emitted, proceeds along its trajectory route, followed by particles of gunpowder that cause a "tattooing," which becomes embedded in the skin of the victim, provided, of course, that the shot was fired from a fairly close range. A soft cloud of soot can often be found on the hand of the person who fired the weapon.

The Murder Investigation

The Five "W"s

The five "W"s are what a murder investigator must attempt to ascertain.

• WHO is the victim: What kind of person was he or she? What were his or her family background, occupation, addictions, sexual preferences, finances? And Who is the possible suspect? A male? A female? A stranger, a friend, a business associate, an employee, an employer, a sexual partner, a family member?

• WHERE did the murder take place? Where the body is found? Was it brought here after the victim was killed or is this the actual scene of the crime?

• WHEN was the crime committed? Day or night? What time? Does the time of death fit any suspects' windows of opportunity?

• WHAT kind of weapon or device was used to kill the victim? A gun, a knife, poison? Did the victim die of smothering, strangulation, hanging, torturing? The weapon or device the assailant used can often point the investigator in a direction that at least helps determine whether the offender was a male or a female. It would take a pretty powerful female to strangle or smother a healthy male victim, but she could strangle or smother another female. Torture? Highly unlikely for a female assailant.

• WHAT brought about the murder? Was it the result of the victim's social, financial, marital, or sexual problems; a robbery or burglary in progress; an argument; or perhaps any one of the possible motives listed in the next section of this book, Motives for Murder?

Motives for Murder

Although most murders have motives, even though they may not always be clear-cut or apparent, unforeseen circumstances may come into play and result in a homicide. For example, a criminal homicide may occur because of:

- Rape
- Robbery
- Burglary
- Larceny
- Motor vehicle theft
- Arson
- Prostitution or other sex offenses
- Drug deals
- Abortion
- Gambling
- Love triangles
- Brawling while consuming alcohol or drugs
- Financial or other arguments
- Street-gang activities
- Organized-crime activities
- Sniper attacks
- Children playing with guns
- Gun cleaning
- Bad drugs

Then there are killings committed by those who are mentally ill or unstable. For example, certain mental illnesses can result in a criminal homicide where an actual motive is nonexistent. Compulsion, as introduced in the famous Leopold and Loeb case, was both a motive and a plea: The killers claimed to have a compulsion to commit murder and, although they were consciously aware that they were committing a heinous act of murder, they claimed that they were mentally and physically unable to stop themselves. Other mental illnesses that have resulted in great tragedies include impulsion, wherein the individual is seized with an urge to commit murder, and paranoia and schizophrenia.

Recently another mental disorder has come to light. It is known as "attachment disorder." Symptoms of this disorder, which seemingly affect mostly adopted children or children from foster homes who suffered abuse and neglect during their formative years, include inner rage and hatred, the inability to love and trust, and the ability to hurt themselves or others without any remorse.

⁍ ⁍ ⁍ ⁍ ⁍

To write about lethal violence, we must first attempt to understand it. Lethal violence is very complex and, although volumes of information would be required to fully understand it, let me attempt to simplify it as much as I possibly can.

First, we must attempt to understand why some violent acts become lethal. Homicide is not one single event. In many cases, there is a large and varied assortment of reasons for the eventual act of taking a human life. For example, domestic violence is more often less lethal than the violence that began as a robbery or a gangland confrontation or a barroom brawl. Each homicide syndrome has its own variance as to its escalation into a homicide.

The offender's intended goal or intended victim is the relevant consideration, i.e., if an innocent bystander comes into the line of fire during a street-gang shooting, the homicide syndrome would still be labeled "street gang."

Expressive versus Instrumental describes the immediate motive of the offender in a violent situation. In instrumental violence, the assailant's primary motive is to steal money or property, while in expressive violence, the primary motive is violence itself.

The following is a partial list of the more general motives for murder:

- Abuse
- Blackmail
- Compulsion
- Debt
- Drugs
- Elimination of competition/Ambition
- Fear of exposure
- Framing
- Hatred
- Human sacrifice
- Impulsion
- Inheritance
- Insurance
- Jealousy
- Justification
- Love
- Mercy
- Passion
- Personal gain
- Preventing a situation
- Revenge
- Sadism
- Serial killing
- Thrill
- To cover another crime

Let's examine some of the motives that lead to criminal homicides.

ABUSE:

(1) Murder is committed while in the act of abusing a spouse, a child, or a parent.

(2) A killer seeks retaliation for having been abused.

BLACKMAIL:

(1) At its simplest and most logical level, an individual would kill his or her blackmailer.

(2) Then again, someone other than the blackmailer's victim might murder the blackmailer to get control of whatever the blackmailer had in his or her custody.

COMPULSION: Killing because of a mental imbalance that causes the killer to kill despite the fact that he or she is aware of committing an illegal and immoral act.

DEBT: Someone heavily in debt would undoubtedly have a motive for murder. The question is who would the victim be?

(1) A person to whom the money is owed? A debt cannot be repaid, so the debtor has no alternative but to kill the person to whom he or she is indebted.

(2) A person is owed a debt that the debtor cannot repay. So the debtor is killed, possibly to set an example to others.

(3) Someone kills to get what is needed to repay a debt.

(4) A debtor repays an outstanding debt by killing someone.

DRUGS: Many motives are associated with drugs—with taking them, selling them, stealing them, being under their influence. Drug homicides can be broken down into three categories:

(1) A drug-related homicide can be considered psychopharmacological when it is the consequence of the perpetrator's or the victim's short- or long-term ingestion of a substance that causes such mood changes in the perpetrator or the victim that would lead to (a) courage to commit a murder, (b) irrational or violent behavior, or (c) the individual's own victimization.

(2) Economic-driven compulsive violence occurs when drug users are compelled to deal in violence in order to support costly habits.

(3) A drug-related homicide is considered systemic with the system of drug use and drug distribution when it is committed as a means of enforcing normative codes, retaliation in drug deals, settling disputes over territory, or punishment for selling phony drugs or for failure to pay drug-related debts.

ELIMINATION OF THE COMPETITION/AMBITION: Seeking to get ahead by taking another's life.

(1) Killing a superior or someone who stands in the way of one's advancement.

(2) Profiting in some way by the death of another.

(3) Drawing attention to oneself as a reporter or a police officer by "reporting" or "discovering" one's own acts of murder and perhaps framing another for those acts.

FEAR OF EXPOSURE: Committing murder to prevent being exposed as the perpetrator of a crime or an incriminating act.

FRAMING: Committing a murder in order to frame an innocent individual or killing someone with the intent of making it appear as if another, who can easily be identified, is responsible for the crime.

HATRED: Racial or religious hatred can bring about a killing. Hatred may lead to the killing of someone or some group that the killer believes is responsible for the destruction of his or her life or that of a loved one. Murderous hatred can be brought about by envy, jealousy, a deep desire to seek revenge, etc.

HUMAN SACRIFICE: Offering up a human being as a religious or cult practice.

IMPULSION: A mentally ill individual murders on an irresistible impulse but without any specific motive.

INHERITANCE: Committing a murder or series of murders in order to claim an inheritance.

INSURANCE:

(1) Killing to collect the insurance money.

(2) Making a suicide appear to be murder in order to collect the insurance.

(3) Assuming the identity of the beneficiary in order to collect the insurance.

(4) Insuring another or others, naming oneself as beneficiary, and then killing them for their insurance.

(5) Pretending to be deceased in order to collect one's own insurance through a plan conceived with another individual.

JEALOUSY: This is a particularly common motive that can be applied easily to situations that involve romance, ambition, and celebrity. It is an emotional or psychological motivation based on envy or the threat of losing a meaningful possession or love. The victim could be the one who threatens to take away that which the jealous person wishes to possess. The victim could be the object of jealousy who is killed to prevent anyone else from possessing him or her.

JUSTIFICATION: Even if a homicide is justifiable or excusable, it still has a motive. Generally, the motive is self-protection. A major difference between a justifiable homicide and a criminal homicide is that, in (most) justifiable homicides, those involved are strangers, while in (most) criminal homicides, the killer and the victim are acquainted.

LOVE: It is highly unlikely that anyone would purposely murder someone they loved unless it was a crime of passion or a mercy killing, where one individual could not stand to see the person he or she so loved continue to suffer without any chance of a cure. Other motives might include one lover being unable to live without the person he or she loves but who has left him or her. Perhaps one lover plans to die or is dying and insists on taking the life of the other.

MERCY: (see LOVE)

PASSION: Passion is an extreme emotion, one of hate, love, and strong desire. One could be passionately ambitious or sexually aroused by another. One could be passionate about a feeling, a belief, even a subject. And then of course there is love. Should passion be the motive, it could have been aroused by sudden rejection or by finding out that a loved one is cheating. Passion could bring about a murder/suicide by an individual who can't see living without the some particular other person. Passion could be the motive for someone who seeks to protect or defend something they believe in strongly, be it right or wrong in the eyes of others.

PERSONAL GAIN: A general catchall for one who kills to achieve or profit in some way from taking the life of his or her victim.

PREVENTING A SITUATION: Killing to ensure that some unpleasant or unwanted situation does not occur.

REVENGE: This could encompass many types of revenge.

(1) An employee wants to get back at his superior or other employees who might have been responsible for his or her loss of a job, a possible raise, or a promotion.

(2) An ex-boyfriend or ex-girlfriend, or wife or husband, blames the other partner for a breakup or for cheating.

(3) A son or a daughter seeks to "get even" for a real or perceived, deserved or undeserved, punishment or for some grief that a parent brought on that child.

(4) An individual seeks to get back at someone who cheated, stole, lied about, or in some way was responsible for the ruination of that individual's life or for the life or lives of others.

SADISM: Murder committed by someone who is obviously mentally disturbed and thrives on torture and sadistic death.

SERIAL KILLING: A series of killings committed by (a) Sociopaths bent on killing to supposedly purify the world of people the sociopaths believe are harmful to society; (b) Compulsive serial killers who hear voices telling them who and when to kill; (c) Power/control killers who seek to display their "superiority" by exercising their "power" over their victims.

Practically all serial killings are based on fantasies. Many serial killings involve dismemberment, mutilation, cannibalism, certain mysterious customs, and the practice of leaving certain markings on the victim. Many times, the serial killer can only get his or her sexual gratification by killing, and some serial killers can only get their sexual gratification by having sex with their victims after they are dead. (See the Serial Killers chapter.)

THRILL: A killer with no regard for human life may possess a premeditated desire to take the life of another or others for the sheer thrill or power of assassinating individuals.

TO COVER ANOTHER CRIME: An individual may kill to silence someone who has knowledge about that individual's commission of another crime. An individual may kill to mislead investigators about his or her involvement in another crime.

LAW ENFORCEMENT

Although there are innumerable law enforcement agencies and departments throughout the country, homicide investigations are, with some minor exceptions, under the jurisdictions of city, county, and state police.

However, there are times when the Federal Bureau of Investigations will investigate or participate in a criminal homicide, especially when it deals with an act of terrorism (such as the Oklahoma City bombing) or a kidnapping, which is a federal offense if the kidnapping was interstate and resulted in murder.

The military services do investigate criminal homicides and, with the exception of the CID (the Army's Criminal Investigations Department), all the other services not only investigate but prosecute as well. The CID turns its cases over to the Judge Advocate's Office for prosecution.

This, of course, does not mean that other law enforcement agencies, including Interpol, do not aid and assist in criminal investigations conducted by local authorities when they are invited to do so.

Interpol, the International Criminal Police Organization, which consists of police forces from its 136 member nations, is not an investigative law enforcement agency. Its purpose is to gather and process information and cooperate in helping to solve important international criminal cases. It manages a criminals-records system of more than 3.3 million names of international criminals, case files, fingerprints, mug shots, and indexes covering boats, airplanes, ships, and other objects used in connection with crimes. It also issues more than a thousand wanted notices each year. It has no written agreements or treaties and does not have the power to search and seize, arrest, or conduct an actual criminal investigation, yet should a murder suspect flee the country or be of foreign extraction, Interpol can play a large part in tracking down the suspect.

HITS: Homicide Investigation & Tracking System

HITS is a computerized murder and sexual assault investigation program that collects and analyzes information pertaining to specific serious criminal offenses. The program's data files, collected from law enforcement agencies all over the country, possess specific information on incidents involving murder, attempted murder, random killing, missing persons, suspected foul play, unidentified murder victims, and predatory sex offenders. HITS also offers information on evidence, victimology, offender characteristics, offender methods of operation, geographic locations of cases, and weapons and vehicles used. In addition, the program offers identification of known murderers and sex offenders in a particular community and an analysis of murder cases that identifies possible links between a single victim, an offender, or cases involving similar violence.

Having ready access to information about such crimes is an important investigative tool for a homicide investigator, especially if such HITS information can provide leads that in turn help solve cases the detective is working on.

An investigator could query the database on:

- Gender
- Race
- Lifestyle
- Date and cause of death

- Location of body
- Presence or absence of clothing
- Concealment of body

Although HITS may not be of much use in certain murder cases, such as domestic murders or ones that carry a specific motive by a specific individual, HITS is especially helpful in cases involving serial killers, professional hit men, organized-crime murders, multiple murders, sexual-assault murders, robbery murders, or a series of homicides that bear a similarity to more than one particular case and for which there doesn't appear to be a suspect that police can connect to the victim.

For more information on the HITS program, contact the National Institute of Justice, U.S. Department of Justice, Office of Justice Programs, Washington, DC.

Tips from a Top Investigator

Writers should note that the use of or lack of use of the following investigative procedures would show the competency of your investigator or, should you prefer, the lack of competency of the official investigator and the intelligence or cleverness of your private investigator.

(1) Always look for signs of a struggle, even if not at first evident.

(2) If a body is in an isolated location, always conduct a spiral search pattern, using the body as the central point.

(3) Look for the entrance and departure paths of the suspect.

(4) Look for other bodies.

(5) Never release a body to the coroner until it has been examined from every angle and steps have been taken to sketch and photograph it. Once a pristine body is removed, it's gone forever.

(6) Always look up when at a crime scene. Clues or evidence of some kind that could be invaluable to the investigator may be on the ceiling or high up on the walls.

(7) Always check on the position of the body—face up, down, sideways. Then check the stains of blood, saliva, vomit, feces, semen for size and direction of flow. It is possible that blood or contaminants flowed in what is apparently the wrong direction. The amount of blood should also be determined—if the amount of blood isn't consistent with the wound, it could easily reveal that the victim was murdered elsewhere and then brought to the spot where the body was found.

(8) If blood froth is coming from the mouth and/or the nose of the victim, it demonstrates that the victim was still breathing after the initial assault with the weapon.

(9) Investigators at a crime scene should always check stairs, entries, hallways, passageways, doors (locked or unlocked), windows (locked, bolted, broken, tool-marked); the kitchen (stove, food on table, settings, glasses or utensils that have been used for possible secretion, shelves, cabinets, interior of refrigerator, lights/lamps for possible fingerprints); the mailbox and its contents, latest newspapers; any diary, address book, appointment book; credit card charges for items purchased or restaurants dined at along with dates; heat or air conditioning that could affect how soon the body temperature of the victim cooled or the effect of confined heat; odors of perfume, aftershave, tobacco, alcohol; ashtrays and contents, waste-paper baskets and outdoor garbage cans; missing garments; bathroom medicine chest, hamper, drains, closets; clothes and pockets of garments; suitcases; safes, disorder or damages done to locations; notes and notepads (indented writing); places of concealment; club memberships; parking tickets; theater tickets; the victim's vehicle, amount of gas left in tank (indicating any possible long trips recently), vehicle glove compartment and trunk.

(10) Always check the victim's hands, especially if the victim is in the state of rigor mortis or if the victim appears to have gone into rigor mortis. For example, the victim may have tightened his or her muscles at the time he or she was killed and the muscles in the hand went into spasm. It is entirely possible that the closed hand of the victim might be holding something—a button, a ring, some evidence that could lead to a suspect or motive.

(11) Get an approximate time of death as quickly as possible. This can aid the investigator in establishing a suspect's opportunity to have committed the murder or establish an alibi for the suspect.

(12) Once all evidence has been collected and a scientific reconstruction of the crime scene has been made, it is time for profiling (see the

next chapter for a discussion of profiling), should the investigator deem it to be a value in his or her investigation.

In the Event the Crime Appears to Have Been Committed Outdoors

The investigator would check:

(1) The weather conditions at the time of death and up to the time when the discovery of the body was made. Much evidence or bloodstains could be changed or lost by precipitation, fog, heat from the sun, snow, etc.

(2) Footprints, vehicle tire tracks, damage to vegetation (grass, bushes, trees, broken twigs), and if in a vegetated area, any possible clothing, fibers, or bloodstains on vegetation caused by the victim's death or the fleeing suspect. Samples of dirt or soil should be taken to match to the suspect's shoes or clothing when the suspect is apprehended.

(3) If the crime scene is discovered and investigated outdoors at night, the investigation may either be postponed until daylight or until proper illumination can be brought in. Officers should be warned not to venture into areas not suitably lit for fear of damaging or destroying evidence not seen in the dark.

In the Event the Victim's Body Has Been Disfigured, Altered, or Is Just Skeletal Remains

Naturally, the investigation of a body that has been burned, decapitated, disfigured, altered, or mutilated makes the role of the investigator much more difficult. How much of the body was mutilated, disfigured, or altered by the killer, and how much by erosion or hungry animals, especially if the body was left above ground or became fish food when immersed in water?

If the body was left above ground, it may have been dragged or moved by roaming animals, so the investigator cannot be sure that where the body was found was where the murder occurred or if the victim was not murdered elsewhere and then brought to where he or she was discovered.

Of great importance is whether the victim still is dressed and whether some of the victim's clothing remains at the scene. Clothing or pieces of clothing could lead to the clothing's manufacturer, the retailers where it is sold, and then to the customer, helping to identify the victim. Any jewelry that the victim may still be wearing or any tattoos, scars, birthmarks could also help identify him or her.

A search should be launched for anything that may have been used to transport the body—ropes, sacks, sheets, etc.—to where it was found if the victim appears to have been killed elsewhere and then brought to the location where the body was found. A search should also be launched for anything that the killer(s) might have dropped or left behind when bringing the victim to this location or leaving the scene.

When the victim's remains are merely skeletal, it becomes extremely difficult to identify them and search for a killer—steps must be made not only to identify the remains but to determine the period of time when the victim was murdered. Remains may be found under water, under floors, buried deep in the earth (and possibly buried alive), in alcoves, or just above the ground, partially covered by moss or vegetation. The fact that a body's remains are skeletal could be attributed to time, the elements, and animals and insects. (See the Crime Lab chapter regarding the crime lab's role in attempting to identify remains and reconstruct facial characteristics from a skull.)

The Profiler

Profiling is virtually a new art in criminal investigations. Although the Federal Bureau of Investigation began the study of profiling somewhere in the mid 1970s, that was almost twenty-five years after psychiatrist Dr. James A. Brussel, known as the Sherlock Holmes of the couch, assisted the N.Y. Police Department in capturing the most-wanted man in the city—The Mad Bomber—by practically drawing a picture of him.

In the early 1980s, The National Center for the Analysis of Violent Crime, located near the FBI Academy, began sharing their think-tank data. This data later became part of a computerized program into which was fed all kinds of information regarding those who committed violent crimes and serial killings.

Today, almost every major law enforcement agency has what is known as a "Profiler," usually a psychologist with a degree in abnormal psychology and criminal profiling. The profiler can often be of great assistance to investigators by providing them with a mental (and practically a physical) picture of the type of individual who would commit a murder of the type that the investigators are investigating and, possibly, offer some suggestions about the motive the killer might have had that is far and away from the usual domestic, business-related, or romantically incited motives.

If possible, the profiler will exhaust all efforts to determine the intelligence and mental alertness of the killer, especially if the killer is a serial killer. Much information can be obtained through VICAP, the Violent Criminal Apprehension Program, a computer databank into which police departments all over the country enter all data related to violent crimes committed in their cities. This program is capable of matching up certain ordinarily undetected similarities between different crimes.

The profiler (sometimes referred to as a behavioral scientist) studies the crime scene and the victim, especially the means by which the victim was murdered; the type of weapon that was used; whether the victim was in any way mutilated; whether their was sex involved with the murder and, if so, the type of sexual encounter that took place and whether the sexual act took place before or after the victim was murdered. Also important is the time the murder took place—the day, the month, the hour.

From the answers to these questions, the profiler can often draw some conclusion about the type of person who would have committed a given act, along with a possible motive, enabling the profiler to tell the investigator what was intended by this act and to construct some sense of motive from the murderer's behavior patterns. This might well reveal the offender's fantasy (and predict any future attempts by the offender to continue his or her fantasy) or the emotional drive that is motivating the offender's ongoing killings. It might also reveal the type of likely future victims, as well as locations, times, and conditions under which future killings could occur.

All of this is hardly guesswork or intuition; it is based on statistical and typological studies that help tell the profiler whether the killer and the victim knew one another and whether the killer picked his or her subject at random or if there was something about the victim that drew the killer to the victim.

Although most murders are either domestic in nature or business- or romance-related, a substantial number of killings can be attributed to those who suffer from major mental and behavioral disorders. Of this group, a large number are sociopathic, sadistic, and narcissistic individuals. Many times, the profiler can offer very strong insights into the killer by considering the type of killing and certain psychological or physical clues the killer left behind at the crime scene.

On occasion, the killer will purposely leave behind something that identifies himself or herself, but not by name, of course. When that is the case, the serial killer wants it to be known that he or she was responsible for the death of the victim(s). It might be the absence of something that ordinarily should be at the crime scene. Or it might be the position or condition in which the killer has left his victim. It might be the type or age of the victim that the killer selects—what it was that attracted the killer to this victim, what or whom the victim represented to the killer. All of these could help direct the investigation and reveal the killer's purposes. Certain types of mutilation or dismemberment also can often indicate what type of person the killer is and from what personality disorder the killer suffers.

With the rapid advancements being made every day in the world of computers, profiling is no longer limited to the work of human profilers. Computers are programmed with specific questions, and once these questions are answered, the computer can develop a classification or a description of the type of individual who is committing the crimes being investigated.

A PROFILER CHECKLIST

The answers to many of the following questions can be of great help in determining the character and personality traits of the suspect and, quite possibly, some reason for the suspect's strong desire or ability to kill.

(1) Is the suspect intelligent?
(2) Is the suspect able to compete socially and sexually with others?
(3) What mood swings does the suspect display?
(4) Is the suspect mobile?
(5) Does the suspect appear to follow media coverage?
(6) What kind of childhood did the suspect have?
(7) Was the suspect an only child?
(8) Was the suspect an abused child?
(9) What are the backgrounds of the suspect's parents, friends, and schoolmates?
(10) Does the suspect keep news clippings and photographs of his victims?

(11) Does the suspect attend his victims' funerals?
(12) Does suspect live alone, with a roommate, a sexual partner, or his parents?
(13) Is the suspect a police groupie?
(14) Does the suspect take any medication?
(15) Does the suspect take drugs?
(16) Is the suspect addicted to alcohol?
(17) Is the suspect a day person or night person?
(18) Does the suspect consider himself or herself a religious person?
(19) Does the suspect keep a diary, notes, or records pertaining to crime?
(20) Is the suspect homosexual or heterosexual?
(21) Is the suspect organized or a helter-skelter killer?
(22) Does the suspect like to leave tantalizing clues or notes behind?
(23) Does the suspect use restraints on his or her victims?
(24) Does the suspect target victims or pick them at random?
(25) Does the suspect have any special victim requirements?
(26) Does the suspect degrade his victims before killing them?
(27) Is the suspect a loner?
(28) Is the suspect employed?
(29) What is suspect's economic status?
(30) Does the suspect have any particular likes: reading, movies, music?

The Private Investigator & the Bounty Hunter

In real life, few private investigators get involved in a homicide. Most of their work is on divorce cases, industrial espionage and counter-espionage, insurance fraud, background checks, domestic relations, locating missing persons, theft investigations, accident claims, and investigations of embezzlement, fraud, forgery, and swindles.

Not so, of course, in crime fiction. Since the days of Sherlock Holmes, the private eye has become the guy who often beats the law at their own game, solving the murder before the local cop even knows what's going on.

The Life of the TV, Film, and Fiction Private Eye Is Murder!

The unofficial investigator, be he or she a P.I. or just an amateur sleuth, has a much more difficult job than a police detective, especially in a homicide case. To be blunt, the P.I. or amateur has no clout, which probably makes for a more interesting murder mystery, since the P.I. or the amateur sleuth has to be much more creative and improvisational. For the P.I. or the amateur sleuth:

≤ Gaining access to evidence is extremely difficult.

≤ Discovering any evidence and not immediately turning it over to the police or knowing the whereabouts of a missing witness or a suspect and not notifying the police is a crime unto itself.

≤ Remember, the crime scene has already been worked over so, even if the P.I. manages to get onto the crime scene after the police have left, there's little to discover.

≤ If the P.I. is working for the defense, you can bet the prosecuting attorney is not going to be very cooperative.
≤ If the police catch a P.I. doing something that even technically infringes upon the law, the license can go bye-bye.

How does the P.I. overcome some of these problems or, better still, how do you get *your* P.I. to skirt these problems?
• Have the P.I. have a friend on the force.
• Have the P.I. discover the murder or be the first one on the scene.
• Have the P.I. pretend not to be a P.I. in order to get witnesses or others to talk. (Maybe he or she can pretend to be a close friend of a relative of the deceased.)

Among the great radio and TV and movie detectives who were not cops but went around solving murders:
Archer
Boston Blackie
Cannon
Charlie Chan
Nick Charles (The Thin Man)
Charlie's Angels
Richard Diamond
Mike Hammer
Hart and Hart
Barnaby Jones
Martin Kane
Magnum
Mannix
Phillip Marlow
Perry Mason
McMillan and Wife
Mr. & Mrs. North
Ellery Queen
Rockford
The Saint
Spenser

Dan Tana
Nero Wolfe

What made and continues to make most of these private eyes so fascinating? Well, one reason is that a P.I. or an amateur sleuth is the little guy next to the cop, and people like to root for the little guy. Another reason is that P.I.'s and amateur sleuths are much more romantic characters, and readers and audiences can more easily identify with them than they can with cops. Remember, too, that the P.I. or the amateur sleuth is the guy (or girl) who is out there on the limb, caught between the good guys and the bad.

(1) They should be very unusual, somewhat offbeat, and interesting characters.
(2) They don't have to concern themselves with the regularities and procedures that law enforcement officers must deal with.
(3) They are often more exposed to danger than the police detective.
(4) Then again, they didn't and most still don't have the facilities, equipment, and the officialdom that law enforcement has to work with. Thus, P.I.'s cannot get warrants. Illegally entering a suspect's or a victim's apartment, business, hotel room, etc., can lead to an arrest for breaking and entering, burglary, and interfering with a police investigation. In essence they have to go around to the back door, sneak around, step over the legal line, and pick up information the best way they can, using every trick and device they can think of to get the job done.
(5) And lastly, not carrying a badge, they're much more vulnerable to getting killed by the bad guy or busted by the law for interfering with a police investigation.

Although some states do not require a P.I. to carry a license, most states do, and securing a P.I.'s license depends on where the P.I. is operating or has set up shop. States that require a license to operate as a private investigator grant licenses through various agencies, depending on the state. In some states, they can be granted by either the State Police or the Secretary of State, while other states require going through the License and Permit Division, the Department of Registration, the

Bureau of Criminal Investigations, the Department of Public Safety, the Office of the Attorney General, the City Licensing Commission, or the local police department. Each state has certain rules that, if disobeyed, can cause the permit or license to be revoked.

Some, but not all, private investigators carry arms, and, depending on the state in which the P.I. is operating, a permit is usually required to do so. When a P.I. crosses into another state, he should notify the proper authorities because his permit does not legally allow him to operate in other states or to carry a weapon into state in which he is not duly licensed.

BOUNTY HUNTERS

Believe it or not, bounty hunters usually have more leeway in crossing state lines than P.I.'s do. In fact, bounty hunters are given more freedom in capturing an escaped felon or a criminal who has jumped bail and fled.

Recently, however, bounty hunters have come under investigation by law enforcement agencies because on more than one occasion, bounty hunters, in quest of escaped felons, have gone to wrong addresses and broken into the homes of innocent people, shooting and, in certain instances, killing them. Law enforcement agencies are now requesting legislation demanding that bounty hunters receive special training, become licensed, and inform local law enforcement of their arrival and the name, address, and charge of the felon they are pursuing. As of this writing, no laws addressing law enforcement's requests have been passed, but this issue is due to go before the legislature in the near future.

· · · · ·

There is a large gap between what is fact and what is fiction. What license you take with your character and what he or she does in your book or script is up to you. *But never confuse dramatic license with logic!* In other words, dramatic license stretches logic, it does not ignore it. A story can easily lose all credibility if an author completely ignores logic in the course of helping his characters achieve their goals and overcome obstacles.

The Homicide Investigation: The Crime Scene

Once the crime scene of a homicide has been investigated, you can never really go back again—at least, not to visit it the way it was. The body has been removed, furniture and other articles have been moved, and the scene has now been trod upon by heaven knows how many officers and technicians. That is why it is so important that every detail of the homicide be noted—measurements taken, ballistics (trajectory of the bullets if shots were fired) sketched, and photographs taken (and even a videotape made) along with the forensic investigation and the gathering of any physical evidence the way it was first discovered.

When a homicide is discovered, the discovery is usually made by a uniformed officer who has been summoned to the scene by a call indicating that a body has been found, there is some evidence of foul play, shots were fired, screams were heard, a call for help was heard, or possibly the foul odor that emanates from a corpse that has been decaying for days becomes very prominent.

Because of recent Supreme Court rulings, a search warrant may be necessary to enter the premises unless the officer secures permission from the property owner or property manager where the suspected homicide has been deemed to have taken place.

That officer, referred to as "the first officer on the scene," has a number of immediate responsibilities. First, he must secure the crime scene, making sure it is cordoned off and that no one goes onto the crime scene or touches anything that could possibly be related to the homicide. He must then make sure that any possible witnesses remain, but he must keep them separated so they cannot compare whatever they may have seen or heard. He then quickly notes all he can about the scene—the position of the deceased; any possible witnesses; the time of day; any odors that may permeate the scene; the weather and temperature (temperature is an important consideration in determining the time of death because weather and room or outside temperature could affect the body); and any unusual aspects at, near, or around the scene who could have some relationship to the homicide. He then notifies his sergeant, who in turn notifies the station or division detectives and Robbery/Homicide at headquarters, and the detectives from the station's homicide squad who catch the case are dispatched to the scene.

The first officer on the scene (or another designated uniformed officer) maintains a log of everyone entering and exiting the crime scene.

The investigating officers assigned to the case must attempt to discover the identity of the killer and the identity of the victim. The last twenty-four hours in the victim's life are very important—they can divulge information that could lead to a motive and the identification of the killer. The quicker witnesses are questioned, the less chance they have of forgetting things they saw and heard. Eyewitnesses should be protected so that the killer cannot make an attempt on their lives.

The longer it takes to identify the killer, the greater the chance that the killer can escape. The investigator, in searching for a suspect, must determine both possible motive and opportunity. Both are essential.

The investigators must have keen eyes as they search for any possible lead, clue, or information that could have any possible connection to the murder: tire tracks, footprints, animal tracks, something missing that should be at the scene, something at the scene that should not be there, pressure on a seat, grass, sand, or a notepad that may reveal the impression of writing done on the top page, which has been removed. Investigators should also consider missing pages out of a personal address book, discarded papers in the garbage, documents that could indicate possible motive, etc. Whatever is discovered is either cast or collected and tagged and bagged and sent on to the crime lab.

In order to do all this, the investigators require the assistance of expert technicians and criminalists, which means summoning what and whom they need from the CSU (Crime Scene Unit) in order to gather any and all physical and trace evidence. The medical examiner is then contacted and asked to report to the crime scene.

The detectives then proceed to examine the crime scene, making sure no one but the criminalists and technicians from the CSU enter it. Everything is noted and written down. The position of the body; the condition of the body when it was found; the location of the body when it was found (determining if the body had been moved—had the victim been killed elsewhere and then brought to the location where it was discovered); the wearing apparel of the victim; the position of the clothes the victim had on at the time of death; any scratch marks, tattoos, or defense wounds; open and closed doors, closets, and drawers; the position of windows, shades, and drapes; the condition of the bed if the victim was found in bed; and anything that is present that would not ordinarily be present or anything missing that should be there.

As I wrote earlier, you can't go back, so everything should be noted that could possibly be relevant to the crime. Was robbery involved? Was the murder committed with anger? Was there any attempt to disfigure or mutilate the victim? Was the victim sexually assaulted? Were drugs present? Look and look again and write it down—that's what a good detective would do.

TYPES OF HOMICIDE

Was it a shooting, a poisoning, a drowning, arson, a knifing, a hanging, a garroting, a suffocating? The type of killing is extremely important because the way the investigation by the detectives and the CSU will proceed will depend on the means of the murder and the way and conditions under which the victim was killed. For example, what may appear to have been murder by drowning may later prove to be wrong when the autopsy doesn't reveal any water in the lungs. This could only mean that the victim died of other causes and probably at a different location and then was placed in the water.

Suppose the victim shows signs of having been hanged, and even rope fibers are imbedded in the victim's neck, but the victim was also tortured and poisoned. Only the Medical Examiner can tell what the actual cause of death was. Perhaps the poison didn't work or the torture brought on a heart attack prior to the victim being hanged. Was the victim still alive when the hanging took place or was he or she already dead from the heart attack or the poison? The actual cause of death is most important because it could help indicate a motive and eventually lead to the killer.

If the murder weapon is not found, an immediate search is conducted to locate the weapon and bag it (a paper, not plastic, bag is used because plastic sweats and could destroy any remaining prints). If a probable weapon is found, it is sent to the crime lab for print identification and then, if it is a gun, to firearms identification to determine if that is indeed the weapon responsible for the victim's death. If it is, then detectives will attempt to find out to whom it belonged.

Meanwhile, members of the homicide team begin questioning possible witnesses (not necessarily eyewitnesses). Some are questioned at the scene, and if it appears that a witness is a valuable witness, he or she may be transported to the station for further questioning, along with any possible suspect(s) who might be present. If there is a possible suspect and the suspect is not present, a search begins while a warrant is sought and issued to apprehend said suspect(s) and to bring the suspect(s) in for questioning. At the same time, other "uniforms" are sent around the neighborhood, canvassing the area, seeking any possible witnesses or individuals who may have pertinent information about the victim and/or any possible suspect.

As soon as Homicide arrives on the scene, a "Murder Book" is started by the detective in charge of the case. Every report made by anyone and everyone connected with the case will go into this book, including the notes of the first officer on the scene, forensics, firearms, detectives running the case, and other investigators taking part in the investigation.

The Murder Book

TABLE OF CONTENTS

File #093-[redacted]-[redacted]-[redacted]

DATE		PAGE
12-08-93	Complaint Report..........................	1
12-08-93	Suppl. Report (Lost Hills Station, Deputies M. D[redacted], J. [redacted] - Active/ Additional Information Not Contained in the First Report.................	5
12-03-93	Personal Effects Inventory Re: [redacted] [redacted]...........................	13
12-08-93	Impounded Vehicle Report Re: License #[redacted]...........................	14
12-09-93	Vehicle Registration Response Re: [redacted]..	15
12-14-93	Suppl. Report (Homicide Bureau, Sergeant P. [redacted] and Investigator M. [redacted]) - Active/Investigation Made/Evidence Held/CC #93-111360...........	20
05-10-94	Suppl. Report (Homicide Bureau, Sergeant P. [redacted] and Investigator M. [redacted]) - Active/Additional Information.....	25
05-10-94	Suppl. Report (Homicide Bureau, Sergeant P. [redacted] and Investigator M. [redacted]) - Active/Additional Information.....	27
05-04-94	Flow Chart Diagram........................	30
05-12-94	Suppl. Report (Homicide Bureau, Sergeant P. [redacted] and Investigator M. [redacted]) - Active/Investigation Made/Evidence Held/CC #93-11360.................	31
12-01-93	Firearms Examination Report Re: Receipt #H392545..........................	34
04-28-94	Firearms Examination Report Re: Receipt #H391886..........................	35
08-29-94	Charge Evaluation Worksheet Re: O[redacted], R[redacted].........................	36
07-28-95	Suppl. Report (Homicide Bureau, Sgt. P. [redacted] and Inv. [redacted]) - Active/Investigation Made/ CC#93-11360................................	37

RECORDS & STATISTICS BUREAU'S USE ONLY

COUNTY OF LOS ANGELES
SHERIFF'S DEPARTMENT

COMPLAINT REPORT

DATE 12-08-93 PAGE 1 OF 4

ACTION: ACTIVE ✓ INACTIVE ( ) PENDING ( ) | INDEX INFO Yes ✓ No ( ) | No of Adult Arrests 0 | No of Subject Detentions 0 | URN (File No) 093-[redacted]

CLASSIFICATION: MURDER 187 PC

CLASSIFICATION: | If Domestic Violence: Weapon Used ( ) YES ( ) NO

DATE TIME DAY OF OCCURRENCE: 12-08-93, 1346, WEDNESDAY | PRINT DEPUTY REQUESTED NO ( ) YES ✓ LOC ✓ STA ( ) VEH ✓ | VIA SECTY BY HOMICIDE | TIME –

LOCATION OF OCCURRENCE: DECKER CYN RD 1.2 MI NORTH OF PACIFIC COAST HWY, MALIBU, 90265 | TYPE OF LOCATION: ROADSIDE TURNOUT | TRACT –

CODE: V—VICTIM, W—WITNESS, I—INFORMANT, R—REPORTING PARTY, P—PARTY. LIST ONE WITNESS (IF NAMED) AND THE INFORMANT ON THIS PAGE.

CODE	LAST NAME	FIRST	MIDDLE	SEX	RACE	DOB
I No 1 of 1	LA CO P.C.O.	UNIT 104M	DAYS			

RESIDENCE ADDRESS: [redacted], B-4[redacted] | CITY | ZIP | RES PHONE (AREA CODE)

BUSINESS ADDRESS: [redacted] AGOURA RD | CITY: AGOURA | ZIP: 91301 | BUS PHONE (AREA CODE): (818) [redacted] ✓

CODE	LAST NAME	FIRST	MIDDLE	SEX	RACE	DOB
No of						

RESIDENCE ADDRESS | CITY | ZIP | RES PHONE (AREA CODE)

BUSINESS ADDRESS | CITY | ZIP | BUS PHONE (AREA CODE)

CODE	LAST NAME	FIRST	MIDDLE	SEX	RACE	DOB
No of						

RESIDENCE ADDRESS | CITY | ZIP | RES PHONE (AREA CODE)

BUSINESS ADDRESS | CITY | ZIP | BUS PHONE (AREA CODE)

CODE: S—SUSPECT, SJ—SUBJECT, M—PATIENT, S/V—SUSPECT/VICTIM, SJ/V—SUBJECT/VICTIM. CIRCLE CODE IF SUPP PAGES USED FOR: V W S SJ M S/V SJ/V

CODE	LAST NAME	FIRST	MIDDLE	DRIVER'S LICENSE (STATE & No)
V No 1 of 1	[redacted]	[redacted]	[redacted]	CA/CD[redacted]

RESIDENCE ADDRESS: [redacted] | CITY: [redacted] | ZIP: [redacted] | RES PHONE (AREA CODE): UNK

BUSINESS ADDRESS: UNK | CITY | ZIP | BUS PHONE (AREA CODE): UNK

SEX	RACE	HAIR	EYES	HEIGHT	WEIGHT	DOB	AGE	WHERE DETAINED OR CITE No
M	H	BLK	BRO	505	165	06-26-55	38	–

OBSERVABLE PHYSICAL ODDITIES: NONE SEEN | AKA NICKNAME: UNK | BOOKING No: –

CLOTHING WORN: BRO JACKET, BLU/WH SHIRT, BLK PANTS, BRO BOOTS, BLK/BRO BELT | MAIN: –

CHARGE: – | WEAPON USED: –

CODE	LAST NAME	FIRST	MIDDLE	DRIVER'S LICENSE (STATE & No)
S No 1 of ?	UNKNOWN			

RESIDENCE ADDRESS | CITY | ZIP | RES PHONE (AREA CODE)

BUSINESS ADDRESS | CITY | ZIP | BUS PHONE (AREA CODE)

SEX	RACE	HAIR	EYES	HEIGHT	WEIGHT	DOB	AGE	WHERE DETAINED OR CITE No

OBSERVABLE PHYSICAL ODDITIES | AKA NICKNAME | BOOKING No

CLOTHING WORN | MAIN

CHARGE | WEAPON USED

VEHICLE USED IN CRIME YES ✓ NO ( ) UNKNOWN ( ) STORED ( ) IMPOUNDED ✓ | YR | MAKE | BODY TYPE | COLOR

LICENSE (STATE & No): – | VIN/FRAME No: –

REGISTERED OWNER: SEE SUPPLEMENTAL REPORT

IDENTIFYING CHARACTERISTICS: –

CHP 180 SUBMITTED YES ✓ NO ( ) | GARAGE NAME & PHONE: –

VICTIM DESIROUS OF PROSECUTION YES ( ) NO ( ) | VICTIM INSURED FOR LOSS YES ( ) NO ( ) | EAP No

SUSPECT/SUBJECT RELEASE APPROVED BY | TIME | ARREST REVIEW SUBMITTED YES ( ) NO ✓

BY DEPUTY: [redacted], M #9 | BADGE No: 23[redacted]

DEPUTY: [redacted], J #7 | BADGE No: 25[redacted]

STATION: LOST HILLS | UNIT/CAR No: 104/31212 | SHIFT: PM'S

APPROVED: SGT. [redacted] | BADGE No: 10[redacted] | 12-9 | TIME: 0224

ASSIGNMENT: HOMICIDE BUREAU

SPECIAL REQUEST DISTRIBUTION

TT B/C BY | DATE | TIME | SECTY: MG 12.9.93

76C300F-SH-R-49 (Rev. 1/86) PS 1/86

(1)

USE FOR PROPERTY NARRATIVE AS NEEDED TAG-149 PAGE 2 OF 4

DATE 12-08-93 | TIME REC'D 1408 | DET ( ) CALL (✓) URN 293-[redacted]

INPUT CHECKED NCIC CII ETC YES ✓ NO ( ) EVIDENCE (CODE-EV) HELD YES ( ) NO ✓ MARKED TAGGED SEALED & PLACED IN STATION EVIDENCE LOCKER INSIDE ( ) OUTSIDE ( ) SAFE ( ) REFRIG ( ) BY LEDGER PAGE No

IF BURGLARY FORCE USED YES ( ) NO ( ) POINT OF ENTRY-DOOR ( ) WINDOW ( ) ROOF ( ) OTHER

PROPERTY (TOTAL VALUE) RECOVERED $ 0 STOLEN $ 0 DAMAGED $ 0

PROPERTY CODE: S—stolen R—recovered L—lost F—found E—embezzled D—damaged (Use All Applicable Codes. For Example, If Property Is Both Stolen & Recovered, Code Is S/R) PROPERTY RELEASED TO

CODE	ITEM No	QUAN	DESCRIPTION — INCLUDE KIND OF ARTICLE, TRADE NAME, IDENTIFYING NUMBERS, PHYSICAL DESCRIPTION, MATERIAL, COLOR, CONDITION, AGE AND PRESENT MARKET VALUE	SERIAL No.	VALUE
					$

AT 1408 HRS WE RECEIVED A CALL OF AN ABANDONED VEHICLE AT DECKER CYN RD, 1.2 MILES NORTH OF PACIFIC COAST HIGHWAY.

WE ARRIVED AT 1441 HRS AND SPOKE TO PARKING CONTROL OFFICER [redacted] (UNIT 104M). HE TOLD US THAT HE RECEIVED A CALL OF AN ABANDONED VEHICLE AT THE LOCATION AT 1300 HRS. HE ARRIVED AT THE LOCATION AT 1346 HRS AND CHECKED THE VEHICLE WHICH WAS PARKED ON THE SIDE OF THE ROAD.

[redacted] SAW A MALE (LATER IDENTIFIED AS THE VICTIM) LAYING DOWN INSIDE THE VEHICLE. ENCINAS

SCREENING FACTORS

YES	NO		YES	NO	
	✓	1. SUSPECT IN CUSTODY		✓	7. GENERAL SUSPECT DESCRIPTION
	✓	2. SUSPECT NAMED/KNOWN		✓	8. GENERAL VEHICLE DESCRIPTION
	✓	3. UNIQUE SUSPECT IDENTIFIERS	✓		9. UNIQUE M.O. OR PATTERN
	✓	4. VEHICLE IN CUSTODY		✓	10. SIGNIFICANT PHYSICAL EVIDENCE
	✓	5. UNIQUE VEHICLE IDENTIFIERS		✓	11. TRACEABLE STOLEN PROPERTY
✓		6. WRITER/REVIEWER DISCRETION		✓	12. MULTIPLE WITNESSES

PART I STATISTICAL INFORMATION — ADDITIONAL CRIMES 1) ____ 2) ____ NUMBER OF VICTIMS ____

TYPE OF PROPERTY	STOLEN	RECOVERED	TYPE OF PROPERTY	STOLEN	RECOVERED
			JEWELRY	$	$
CLOTHING/FURS	$	$	LIVESTOCK	$	$
CONSUMABLE GOODS	$	$	LOCAL STOLEN VEHICLES	$	$
CURRENCY/NOTES	$	$	MISCELLANEOUS	$	$
FIREARMS	$	$	OFFICE EQUIPMENT	$	$
HOUSEHOLD GOODS	$	$	TV/RADIO/STEREO	$	$

WEAPONS CODE
( ) ARTICLES THROWN
( ) CAUSTIC CHEMICALS
( ) CLUB/BLUNT INSTRUMENT
( ) DRUGS/NOXIOUS GAS
( ) FIRE/EXPLOSIVES
( ) HANDS/FEET/FIST/ETC
( ) KNIFE/CUTTING INSTRUMENT
( ) POISON
(✓) REVOLVER/PISTOL
( ) RIFLE
( ) SHOTGUN
( ) STRANGULATION
( ) VEHICLE
( ) UNKNOWN/OTHER

(2)

REPORT CONTINUATION NARRATIVE | URN 093-[redacted]

ATTEMPTED TO AROUSE THE VICTIM BUT HE DID NOT RESPOND.

DEP [redacted] #24[redacted] UNIT 101 T2 DAYS ARRIVED AT THE LOCATION AT 1419 HRS AND IMMEDIATELY REQUESTED THAT PARAMEDICS RESPOND.

LA CO PARAMEDICS [redacted] AND [redacted] FROM STATION #11 ARRIVED AT 1420 HRS. THEY CHECKED THE VICTIM AND PRONOUNCED HIM DEAD AT 1440 HRS. THE PARAMEDICS LEFT THE LOCATION PRIOR TO OUR ARRIVAL.

AT 1446 LOST HILLS DESK NOTIFIED HOMICIDE DETECTIVE [redacted] OF THE ABOVE INFORMATION PER OUR REQUEST.

[redacted] TOLD US THAT THE PARAMEDICS DID NOT TELL HIM WHAT THE VICTIM'S CAUSE OF DEATH WAS. HE SAID THAT THE PARAMEDICS BELIEVED THAT THE VICTIM HAD A WOUND IN THE CHEST AREA.

WE SAW THE VICTIM LAYING ON THE FRONT FLOORBOARD OF THE VEHICLE. HE WAS ON HIS LEFT SIDE WITH HIS FEET ON THE DRIVER SIDE (WEST) AND HIS HEAD ON THE PASSENGER SIDE (EAST). WE SAW BLOOD INSIDE THE VEHICLE.

76R288M-Sh R 313- PS 10-82

REPORT CONTINUATION NARRATIVE | URN 093-[redacted]

AT 1648 HRS DET J D [redacted] # [redacted] FROM HOMICIDE BUREAU ARRIVED.

DEPUTY CORONER [redacted] # [redacted] ARRIVED AT 1718 HRS AND REMOVED THE VICTIM FROM THE VEHICLE.

WHEN THE VICTIM WAS REMOVED FROM THE VEHICLE, WE SAW WHAT APPEARED TO BE MULTIPLE GUN SHOT WOUNDS ON THE VICTIMS UPPER TORSO.

AT 1900 HRS R [redacted] #10[redacted] FROM THE CRIME LAB ARRIVED.

HOMICIDE SGT M. [redacted] # [redacted] AND DET [redacted] #01[redacted] ARRIVED AT 1945 HRS.

AT 2015 HRS SEVERAL MEDIA PERSONNEL ARRIVED AND PHOTOGRAPHED THE SCENE.

HOMICIDE LT R[redacted] # [redacted] ARRIVED AT 2025 HRS.

DEPUTY CORONER [redacted]N ISSUED PROPERTY RECEIPT #117517 AND TOOK POSSESSION OF THE VICTIM.

THE VICTIM'S VEHICLE WAS IMPOUNDED.

SEE SUPPLEMENTAL REPORT, SAME FILE NUMBER, FOR ADDITIONAL INFORMATION.

76R288M-Sh-R-313- PS 10-82

(4)

765878R-SH-R 77 5-66

COUNTY OF LOS ANGELES – SHERIFF'S DEPARTMENT – SUPPLEMENTARY REPORT

DATE 12-08-93 FILE NO. 093-[redacted]1

C. MURDER 187 PC Action Taken ACTIVE, ADDITIONAL INFORMATION NOT CONTAINED IN THE FIRST REPORT

V [redacted], [redacted] [redacted] MH/06-26-55

CODE	LAST NAME	FIRST	MIDDLE	SEX	RACE	DOB
W No 1 of 3	[redacted]	[redacted]	[redacted]	F	W	A
RESIDENCE ADDRESS		CITY	ZIP	RES PHONE (AREA CODE)		
[redacted]		[redacted]U	90265	(310) 457-4256		
BUSINESS ADDRESS		CITY	ZIP	BUS PHONE (AREA CODE)		
SAME (SELF EMPLOYED)				(310) 457-4257		
W No 2 of 3	[redacted]	[redacted]H	–	M	W	A
RESIDENCE ADDRESS		CITY	ZIP	RES PHONE (AREA CODE)		
[illegible]		[illegible]	[illegible]			
BUSINESS ADDRESS		CITY	ZIP	BUS PHONE (AREA CODE)		
[illegible]		[illegible]	[illegible]	[illegible]		
W No 3 of 3	[redacted]S	[redacted]E	[redacted]	F	W	A
RESIDENCE ADDRESS		CITY	ZIP	RES PHONE (AREA CODE)		
[redacted] DECKER CYN RD		MALIBU	90265	(310) 457-9723		
BUSINESS ADDRESS		CITY	ZIP	BUS PHONE (AREA CODE)		
SAME (RETIRED PARAMEDIC)				–		

CODE: S—SUSPECT, SJ—SUBJECT, M—PATIENT, S/V—SUSPECT/VICTIM, SJ/V—SUBJECT/VICTIM CIRCLE CODE IF SUPP. PAGES USED FOR: V W S SJ M S/V

CODE No OF	LAST NAME	FIRST	MIDDLE	DRIVER'S LICENSE (STATE & No)
RESIDENCE ADDRESS		CITY	ZIP	RES PHONE (AREA CODE)
BUSINESS ADDRESS		CITY	ZIP	BUS PHONE (AREA CODE)
SEX / RACE / HAIR / EYES / HEIGHT / WEIGHT		DOB	AGE	WHERE DETAINED OR CITE No
OBSERVABLE PHYSICAL ODDITIES		AKA NICKNAME		BOOKING No
CLOTHING WORN				MAIN
CHARGE				WEAPON USED

CODE No OF	LAST NAME	FIRST	MIDDLE	DRIVER'S LICENSE (STATE & No)
RESIDENCE ADDRESS		CITY	ZIP	RES PHONE (AREA CODE)
BUSINESS ADDRESS		CITY	ZIP	BUS PHONE (AREA CODE)
SEX / RACE / HAIR / EYES / HEIGHT / WEIGHT		DOB	AGE	WHERE DETAINED OR CITE No
OBSERVABLE PHYSICAL ODDITIES		AKA NICKNAME		BOOKING No
CLOTHING WORN				MAIN
CHARGE				WEAPON USED

VEHICLE USED IN CRIME YES ✓ NO ( ) UNKNOWN ( ) STORED ( ) IMPOUNDED ✓	YR 84	MAKE CHEVY	BODY TYPE P/U	COLOR BLU/WHI	BY DEPUTY [redacted], M #9	BADGE No 23[redacted]
LICENSE (STATE & No) CA/[redacted]		VIN/FRAME No			DEPUTY [redacted], J #7	BADGE No 25[redacted]
REGISTERED OWNER [redacted], [redacted], [redacted]					STATION LOST HILLS — UNIT/CAR No 104/31212	SHIFT PM'S
IDENTIFYING CHARACTERISTICS BLU/WHI CAMPER SHELL					APPROVED SGT. [redacted] BADGE No 1[redacted]4 12-9	TIME 024
CHP 180 SUBMITTED YES ✓ NO ( ) GARAGE NAME & PHONE SIERRA TOW (818) 707-2197					ASSIGNMENT HOMICIDE BUREAU	
VICTIM DESIROUS OF PROSECUTION YES ( ) NO ( ) — VICTIM INSURED FOR LOSS YES ( ) NO ( ) — EAP No					SPECIAL REQUEST DISTRIBUTION	
SUSPECT/SUBJECT RELEASE APPROVED BY — TIME		ARREST REVIEW SUBMITTED YES ( ) NO ✓			TT B/C BY — DATE — TIME	SECTY MG12

76C300F-SH-R-49 (Rev. 1/86)

(5)

REPORT CONTINUATION NARRATIVE | URN 093-[redacted]

WE RESPONDED TO DECKER CYN RD, 1.2 MILES NORTH OF PACIFIC COAST HWY AFTER RECEIVING A CALL OF AN ABANDONED VEHICLE. LOST HILLS DESK INFORMED US THAT THE CALL HAD ORIGINALLY BEEN ASSIGNED TO UNIT 104M (PCO [redacted] # [redacted]) HOWEVER HE DISCOVERED A DEAD BODY INSIDE THE VEHICLE.

I ASKED LOST HILLS STATION DISPATCHER [redacted] # [redacted] WHO THE INFORMANT ON THE CALL WAS. SHE SAID THAT THE CALL HAD BEEN TAKEN BY LOST HILLS DISPATCHER [redacted] # [redacted], DAY SHIFT, HOWEVER [redacted] HAD GONE HOME FOR THE DAY. [redacted] SAID THAT [redacted] SAID THAT THE INFORMANT WAS A PASSERBY WHO SAID THE VEHICLE HAS BEEN AT THE LOCATION FOR DAYS, WITH THE WINDOWS DOWN. THE INFORMANT DID NOT LEAVE THEIR NAME, ADDRESS OR A PHONE NUMBER.

UPON OUR ARRIVAL WE SAW A BLUE/WHITE 84' CHEVY SILVERADO P/U WITH A BLUE/WHITE CAMPER SHELL, CA LIC # 3[redacted] PARKED ON THE EAST SIDE OF DECKER CYN RD IN A DIRT TURNOUT AREA. THE AREA THAT THE TRUCK WAS PARKED IN WAS GRADED AND WAS NOT WIDE ENOUGH TO TURN THE TRUCK AROUND. THE VEHICLE APPEARED TO HAVE BEEN BACKED INTO THE AREA. THE VEHICLE WAS FACING NORTH (UPHILL) AND WAS VISABLE FROM DECKER CYN RD. THE VEHICLE WAS

76R288M-Sh R-313- PS 10-82

REPORT CONTINUATION NARRATIVE | URN 093-[redacted]

APPROX 15-20' EAST OF DECKER CYN RD. WE SAW THAT THE DRIVER SIDE DOOR WAS CLOSED, UNLOCKED AND THE WINDOW WAS ROLLED DOWN. THE PASSENGER DOOR WAS OPEN AND THE WINDOW WAS UP. THE KEYS WERE IN THE IGNITION AND THE MOTOR WAS OFF.

WE SAW THE VICTIM LYING ON HIS LEFT SIDE ON THE FLOORBOARD. HIS FEET WERE ON THE DRIVER'S SIDE (WEST) AND HIS HEAD WAS ON THE PASSENGER SIDE (EAST). WE SAW WHAT APPEARED TO BE BLOOD ON THE PASSENGER, LOWER PORTION OF THE SEAT AND BLOOD ON A CASSETTE TAPE WHICH WAS ON THE CENTER OF THE SEAT. WE ALSO SAW WHAT APPEARED TO BE A SMALL STREAM OF BLOOD COMING FROM UNDER THE VICTIM WHICH RAN OUT THE OPENED PASSENGER DOOR.

[redacted] TOLD US THAT HE ARRIVED AT THE LOCATION AT 1346 HRS AND SAW THE VEHICLE PARKED IN THE SAME LOCATION. WHEN HE WALKED UP TO THE TRUCK, HE SAW THAT THE DRIVER SIDE DOOR WAS CLOSED, UNLOCKED AND THE WINDOW WAS DOWN. HE SAW THAT THE PASSENGER DOOR WAS CLOSED, UNLOCKED AND THE PASSENGER WINDOW WAS UP.

[redacted] SAID THAT HE SAW THE VICTIM LYING IN THE VEHICLE IN THE SAME POSITION THAT WE HAD SEEN HIM WITH THE EXCEPTION OF HIS JACKET AND

7GR288M-Sh R 313- PS 10-82

REPORT CONTINUATION NARRATIVE URN 093-[redacted]

SHIRT, WHICH HAD BEEN PULLED UP BY THE PARAMEDICS WHO ATTACHED EQUIPMENT TO THE VICTIM IN ORDER TO MONITOR HIS VITAL SIGNS. [redacted] SAID THAT THE PARAMEDICS ROLLED THE VICTIM OVER SLIGHTLY TO EXAMINE HIM, BUT THEY DID NOT REMOVE HIM FROM THE VEHICLE.

[redacted] SAID THAT WHEN HE INITIALLY DISCOVERED THE VICTIM, HE ATTEMPTED TO AROUSE HIM BY SHOUTING AT HIM. WHEN HE DID NOT SEE THE VICTIM RESPOND, HE OPENDED THE DRIVER SIDE DOOR AND SHOOK THE VICTIM'S FEET IN AN ATTEMPT TO AROUSE HIM. [redacted] DID NOT SEE ANY RESPONSE. HE WALKED AROUND THE TRUCK AND OPENED THE PASSENGER DOOR AND ATTEMPTED TO LOCATE A PULSE AT THE VICTIM'S NECK. HE DID NOT FEEL A PULSE.

DEP [redacted] #24[redacted], UNIT 101T2 ARRIVED AT THE LOCATION AT 1419 HRS AND IMMEDIATELY REQUESTED THAT PARAMEDICS RESPOND. PARAMEDICS [redacted] AND [redacted] FROM LA CO FIRE STATION #71 ARRIVED AT 1420 HRS AND PRONOUNCED THE VICTIM DEAD AT 1440 HRS. THE PARAMEDICS LEFT THE LOCATION PRIOR TO OUR ARRIVAL.

AT 1450 HRS W-1 [redacted] WAS DRIVING SOUTH ON DECKER CYN RD AND STOPPED AT THE LOCATION. SHE TOLD ME THAT AT APPROX 0930 HRS TODAY SHE WAS DRIVING SOUTH ON DECKER CYN RD AND WAS TURNING

76R288M-Sh A 313- PS 10-82

(8)

REPORT CONTINUATION NARRATIVE | URN 093-[redacted]

EAST ONTO DECKER EDISON RD. FROM THE INTERSECTION OF DECKER CYN RD AND DECKER EDISON RD SHE SAW THE VICTIM'S TRUCK STOPPED IN THE NORTHBOUND LANE OF DECKER CYN RD NEXT TO THE DIRT TURNOUT. W/[redacted] DROVE ON DECKER EDISON RD AND STOPPED AT A POSITION ABOVE THE VICTIM'S TRUCK, APPROX 100' EAST. SHE SAW AN OLDER, BROWN COMPACT VEHICLE (NFD) DRIVE NORTH [illegible] [illegible]. W/[redacted] HEARD THE DRIVER OF THE BROWN VEHICLE SAY "YOU BETTER GET YOUR CAR OUT OF THE ROAD". SHE DISCRIBED THE OCCUPANT OF THE BROWN CAR AS A MALE WHITE OR HISPANIC (NFD). W/[redacted] SAID THAT SHE DID NOT SEE THE VICTIM INSIDE HIS TRUCK, SHE ASSUMED THAT HE WAS OUTSIDE. SHE SHOUTED TOWARD THE VEHICLES AND ASKED IF EVERYTHING WAS OK. THE OCCUPANT OF THE BROWN CAR HAD STEPPED FROM HIS VEHICLE. HE REPLIED "WE ARE FINE, WE ARE FINE". W/[redacted] BELIEVES THAT SHE ALSO SAW THE OCCUPANT OF THE TRUCK STANDING OUTSIDE HIS TRUCK HOWEVER SHE WAS UNABLE TO FURTHER DESCRIBE THE OCCUPANT OF THE BROWN CAR OR THE OTHER PERSON. W/[redacted] CONTINUED TO HER DESTINATION ([redacted] DECKER EDISON RD) AND DID NOT SEE OR HEAR ANYTHING ELSE SUSPICIOUS. W/[redacted] SAID THAT WHEN SHE HEARD THE DRIVER OF THE BROWN CAR SAY "YOU BETTER GET YOUR CAR OUT OF THE ROAD", HE SOUNDED MAD.

HOMICIDE DETECTIVE J D S[redacted] #D[redacted] ARRIVED

76R288M-Sh R 31J- PS 10-82

REPORT CONTINUATION NARRATIVE | URN 093-

AT 1648 HRS AND EXAMINED THE SCENE. WHEN HE OPENED THE VEHICLE'S DRIVER DOOR HE SAW AN EXPENDED SHELL CASING ON THE DRIVER SIDE FLOORBOARD, NEXT TO THE DOOR. THE CASING APPEARED TO BE A .25 CAL.

DEPUTY CORONER ▬ # ▬ ARRIVED AT 1718 HRS AND UNDER THE DIRECTION OF DETECTIVE J D SMITH, REMOVED THE VICTIM FROM THE VECHILE, THROUGH THE DRIVER SIDE DOOR. AFTER THE VICTIM HAD BEEN REMOVED, WE SAW THREE EXPENDED SHELL CASINGS WHICH APPEARED TO BE .25 CAL AND AN EXPENDED BULLET, WHICH ALSO APPEARED TO BE .25 CAL, ON THE PASSENGER SIDE OF THE FLOORBOARD. DETECTIVE J D ▬ DETERMINED THAT THE VICTIM HAD DIED AS A RESULT OF HOMICIDE AT 1735 HRS. HE REQUESTED HOMICIDE/MURDER INVESTIGATORS TO RESPOND.

DETECTIVE J D ▬ FOUND A PASSPORT INSIDE A POUCH ON THE DRIVER'S DOOR. THE PASSPORT CONTAINED A PHOTOGRAPH OF THE VICTIM AS WELL AS HIS NAME AND BIRTHDATE. HE ALSO FOUND AN ENVELOPE, BEHIND THE SEAT WHICH WAS ADDRESSED TO "RESIDENT ▬ ▬ DR, OXNARD, 93030". IT WAS DATED DEC 6.

AT 1730 W2 ▬ WAS DRIVING PAST THE CRIME SCENE, HE STOPPED AND SPOKE TO SGT ▬ # 19▬ (UNIT 2203) WHO WAS ALSO AT THE SCENE. W2 ▬ TOLD SGT ▬

1/2/241 W2 NEWHART

6R288M-Sh R-313- PS 10-82

REPORT CONTINUATION NARRATIVE | URN 093- ██████ 11

THAT AT APPROX 1000 HRS TODAY,
HE AND HIS WIFE (████E) HAD DRIVEN PAST THE LOCATION AND SAW SOMEONE WITH A CHEKERD SHIRT, SITTING IN THE PASSENGER SIDE OF THE TRUCK. THEY SAW THAT THE PERSON WAS MOVING. THEY WERE UNABLE TO PROVIDE ANY FURTHER DESCRIPTION OF THE OCCUPANT INSIDE THE TRUCK. THEY DID NOT STOP, THEY CONTINUED TO DRIVE BY THE TRUCK.

AT 1740 HRS, W3 ███S WAS DRIVING NORTH ON DEKKER CYN RD. SHE STOPPED AND TOLD ME THAT AT APPROX 0940 HRS TODAY, SHE WAS DRIVING SOUTH ON DEKKER CYN RD. SHE SAW THE TRUCK PARKED IN THE TURNOUT, IN THE SAME POSITION AS IT WAS CURRENTLY. SHE DID NOT SEE ANYONE INSIDE OR NEAR THE TRUCK AT 0940 HRS.

A DMV CHECK OF THE VEHICLE'S LICENSE PLATE RETURNED WITH INFORMATION THAT IT IS REGISTERED TO THE VICTIM AT ███ W. ████ ST, HANFORD, 93230.

DETECTIVE JD ███ FOUND AND ADDITIONAL PAIR OF LICENSE PLATES (CA ██████) A DMV CHEK OF THAT LICENSE PLATE RETURNED WITH INFORMATION OF A REGISTERED OWNER OF ████ ████ ████, 1█5 W. ████ ST, HANFORD, 93230 . THE VIN NUMBER

76R288M-Sh R 313 PS 10-82

REPORT CONTINUATION NARRATIVE | URN 093-[redacted]

INDICATED THAT THE LICENSE PLATES WERE ISSUED FOR THE SAME VEHICLE.

DEPUTY CORONER [redacted] MOVED THE VICTIM IN ORDER TO EXPOSE HIS WOUND. I SAW WHAT APPEARED TO BE FOUR GUNSHOT WOUNDS ON THE VICTIM'S UPPER, LEFT BACK AREA AND WHAT APPEARED TO BE A GUNSHOT EXIT WOUND ON THE VICTIM'S UPPER LEFT CHEST AREA.

HOMICIDE SGT [redacted] AND DETECTIVE [redacted] COLLECTED PAPERWORK, KEYS , SHELL CASINGS AND THE EXPENDED BULLET FROM THE VEHICLE AND RETAINED THE ITEMS AS EVIDENCE.

DEPUTY CORONER [redacted] SAID THAT THE CORONERS OFFICE WOULD ATTEMPT TO LOCATE AND INFORM THE VICTIM'S NEXT OF KIN OF THE VICTIMS DEATH.

THE VICTIMS VEHICLE WAS IMPOUNDED PER 22655.5(a)(2) VC AND TOWED TO SIERRA TOW, 2326 TOWNSGATE RD, WESTLAKE VILLAGE, (818) 707-2197. (SEE CHP-180, SAME FILE NUMBER)

76R288M-Sh R 313- PS 10.82

(12)

COUNTY OF LOS ANGELES

PERSONAL EFFECTS INVENTORY

DEPARTMENT OF CORONER

2

1104 . ..th Mission Road, Los Angeles, CA 90033 (213) 343-.

Property Released — Monday through Friday 8:00 AM to 4:00 PM
Closed Saturday, Sunday & Holidays

☐ NO PERSONAL EFFECTS TAKEN ☐ NO CASH TAKEN

☐ ADDITIONAL RECEIPTS # ______

No. 117517
Date 12-3-93
Case # 93-11361
Name [redacted]

PERSONAL EFFECTS: U.S. Cash SIXTY-EIGHT CENTS (.68¢) Dollars

Keepsake/Foreign Monies ELEVEN-HUNDRED TWENTY SEVEN PESOS

Item	No.	Yes.	Qty.	Description	To: Notif	Item	No.	Yes.	Qty.	Number	To: Notif
Wallet						Driver's License					
Purse						Soc. Security					
Misc. Papers						Passport		X	1	MEXICO AFRE 492	
Address						Military I.D./Vet. Card					
Suicide Note						Immig. Card					
Glasses						P.F. Card					
Keys						[illegible]					

The following identification documents are routinely returned to the issuing agencies: California Driver's Licenses, California Identification Cards ... Passports and Military I.D. Cards.

Watches, Jewelry & Other Items	Credit Cards, Traveler's Checks and Checks for Decedent (List bank acct. nos., amount, card name and no.)
Ø	Ø

DECLARATION FOR RELEASE OF WEAPONS IN THE FIELD:
The Dept. of Coroner does not accept firearms. The following (describe) ______ caliber ______ make ______ model ______ type
Weapon bearing serial number Ø was released to: ______ name ______ badge/I.D.#
Name of Agency: ______ Phone Number ( )
Address: ______

WITNESS DECLARATION: UNDER PENALTY OF PERJURY, I DECLARE:
☐ The above list is all the property found on the body, clothing or adjacent area to the above named decedent and was checked by me in the presence of the witnesses signed below.
☐ Above is listed all the property of the above indicated decedent after the body, clothing or adjacent area had been checked prior to my arrival.

Signature [signature] Print Name & Title S. [redacted] #2[redacted]
Witness Sign [signature] Print Name & Title [redacted] DEPUTY SHERIFF
Address & Agency LASD LOST HILLS City ______ ZIP ______ Phone ( )
Witness Sign ______ Print Name & Title ______
Address & Agency ______ City ______ ZIP ______ Phone ( )

DECLARATION FOR RELEASE OF PROPERTY IN THE FIELD:
The above indicated personal effects were released to me by ______ Date ______
Signature ______ Print Name & Title ______
Agency ______ Phone ( )

DECLARATION FOR RELEASE OF PROPERTY TO FAMILY:
The above listed property was delivered to me by ______ of the Property Section of the Dept. of Coroner, Los Angeles County.
Signature ______ Print Name ______
Relationship ______ Date ______ Phone ( )
Address ______ City ______ ZIP ______

PROPERTY WILL NOT BE RELEASED WITHOUT AFFIDAVIT PURSUANT TO SECTION 630 PROBATE CODE OR LETTERS TESTAMENTAR

(13)

DEPARTMENT OF CALIFORNIA HIGHWAY PATROL
VEHICLE REPORT
CHP 180 (REV 4-90) OPI 065 FCN 2329334300623

NOTE: CHP 180 IS FURNISHED TO ALL PEACE OFFICERS BY THE CALIFORNIA HIGHWAY PATROL

REPORTING DEPARTMENT	LOCATION CODE	DATE / TIME OF REPORT	NOTICE OF STORED VEHICLE DELIVERED PERSONALLY	FILE NUMBER
LASO/LOST HILLS FORT	1900-10	12-8-93/2100	☐	093-[redacted]

LOCATION TOWED / STOLEN FROM	ODOMETER READING	VIN CLEAR IN SVS	DATE / TIME DISPATCH NOTIFIED
DECKER CYN RD, 1.2 MI NORTH OF PACIFIC COAST HWY, MALIBU	12108	☒ YES ☐ NO	12-8-93/1259
		LIC CLEAR IN SVS ☒ YES ☐ NO	

YEAR	MAKE	MODEL	BODY TYPE	COLOR	LICENSE NUMBER	☐ ONE ☒ TWO	MONTH / YEAR	STATE
84	CHEVY	SILVERADO	P/U	BLU/WHI	[redacted]		6/94	CA

VEHICLE IDENTIFICATION NUMBER	ENGINE NUMBER	APPRAISED VALUE / OWNER VALUATION
[partially redacted]	—	☐ 0-200 ☐ 201-1000 ☐ 1000- ☒ 3,000

REGISTERED OWNER: [redacted], [redacted] ST, HANFORD, 93230

LEGAL OWNER: (SAME)

☐ STORED ☒ IMPOUNDED ☐ RELEASED ☐ RECOVERED - VEHICLE / COMPONENT

TOWING / STORAGE CONCERN (NAME, ADDRESS, PHONE): SIERRA TOW - 2326 TOWNSGATE RD WESTLAKE VLG. 91361 (818) 707-2197

TOWED TO / STORED AT: SAME

STORAGE AUTHORITY AND REASON: 20655.5(a)(2) VC - EVIDENCE OF CRIME

DRIVEABLE: ☒ YES ☐ NO ☐ UNK

VIN APPEAR ALTERED / REMOVED: ☐ YES ☒ NO

VIN COMPARE WITH REG CARD: ☒ YES ☐ NO

CONDITION	YES	NO	ITEMS	YES	NO	ITEMS	YES	NO	TIRES / WHEELS	CONDITION	ITEMS	IDENTIFICATION NUMBER
WRECKED		✓	SEAT (FRONT)	✓		REGISTRATION		✓	LEFT FRONT	FAIR	CAMPER	SHELL
BURNED		✓	REAR (REAR)		✓	ALT / GENERATOR	✓		RIGHT FRONT	SAME	CARGO	
VANDALIZED		✓	RADIO	✓		BATTERY	✓		LEFT REAR	SAME	VESSEL AS LOAD	
ENG / TRANS STRIP		✓	TAPE DECK	✓		DIFFERENTIAL	✓		RIGHT REAR	SAME	FIREARMS	
MISC. PARTS STRIP		✓	TAPES	✓		TRANSMISSION	✓		SPARE	UNK	OTHER	
BODY METAL STRIP		✓	OTHER RADIO		✓	AUTOMATIC	✓		HUB CAPS	—		
VIN SWITCH		✓	IGNITION KEY	✓		MANUAL		✓	SPECIAL WHEELS	—		

RELEASE VEHICLE TO: ☐ R/O AGENT ☐ AGENCY HOLD

GARAGE PRINCIPAL OR AGENT STORING VEHICLE (SIGNATURE): [redacted]

DATE / TIME: 2100 12-8-93

NAME OF PERSON AUTHORIZING RELEASE | DATE

CERTIFICATION: I, THE UNDERSIGNED, DO HEREBY CERTIFY THAT I AM LEGALLY AUTHORIZED AND ENTITLED TO TAKE POSSESSION OF THE ABOVE DESCRIBED VEHICLE.

SIGNATURE OF PERSON AUTHORIZING RELEASE

SIGNATURE OF PERSON TAKING POSSESSION

☐ STOLEN VEHICLE / COMPONENT ☐ EMBEZZLED VEHICLE ☐ PLATE(S) REPORT

DATE AND TIME OF OCCURRENCE	DATE AND TIME REPORTED	NAME OF REPORTING PARTY	DRIVERS LICENSE NUMBER AND STATE
LAST DRIVER OF VEHICLE	DATE AND TIME	ADDRESS	TELEPHONE ( )

I CERTIFY OR DECLARE UNDER PENALTY OF PERJURY UNDER THE LAWS OF THE STATE OF CALIFORNIA THAT THE FOREGOING IS TRUE AND CORRECT.

SIGNATURE OF PERSON MAKING REPORT | DATE

REMARKS
[LIST PROPERTY, TOOLS, VEHICLE DAMAGE, ARRESTS.]

REPORTED BY: 104/PM'S

VEHICLE IMPOUNDED FOR CRIMINAL INVESTIGATION. R/O INFORMATION OBTAINED FROM PAPERWORK INSIDE VEHICLE AND VERIFIED VIA DMV.

ENTERED INTO SVS. AS IMPOUNDED BY SECRETARY MG AT 0315 HRS. ENTER AS IMPOUND, HELD FOR INVESTIGATION.

SGT. [redacted] #105814

SIGNATURE OF OFFICER TAKING REPORT	I.D. NUMBER	SUPERVISOR	REQUIRED NOTICES SENT TO REGISTERED AND LEGAL OWNERS PER 22852 CVC	DATE NOTIFIED
[redacted], M	[redacted]4	12-9-93 0246	☐ YES ☒ NO	MG 12-9-93

(14)

0?3-[redacted]

PAGE 001 12/09/93 03:12:48 LHSP PRINT REQUESTED BY TERMINAL LHS3
TO: LHS3 FROM: CLETS   12/09/93 03:12:23
IA
QV.CA0190022.LIC/3FGB552.LIS/C
NO HITS

PAGE 002
TO: LHS3 FROM: CLETS   12/09/93 03:12:25
..

DATE: 12/09/93 TIME: 03:10
REG VALID FROM: 06/20/93 TO 06/20/94

LIC#:3FGB552 YRMD:84 MAKE:CHEV BTM :PM
VIN :1[redacted]
R/O :[redacted]Z [redacted]O M[redacted]O, [redacted] [redacted]S ST
CITY:HANFORD C.C.:16 ZIP :93230

PARKING VIOLATIONS: NONE

END

```
PAGE 003
TO: LHS3   FROM: CLETS                          12/09/93  03:12:28
IV


DATE: 12/09/93 TIME: 03:11
REG VALID FROM: 06/20/93 TO 06/20/94
LIC#:3■■■■■2 YRMD:84 MAKE:CHEV BTM :PM VIN :1■■■■■■■■■■■■■■2
R/O :■■■■Z ■■■■■■ ■■■■■■■, ■■■■ W ■■■■■■ ST CITY:HANFORD C.C.:16
ZIP#:93230
RCID:10/27/93 OCID:11/07/93 LOCD:5
TYPE:11 POWR:G VEH :13 BODY:J CLAS:BV *-YR:91
REC STATUS:
10/27/93 VR INSPECTION EXEMPTION
10/27/93 PREV LIC Y■■■■■7


CLEARANCE INFORMATION RECORDS
OFFICE    WORK DATE     TECH/ID     SEQ #     VALUE      FICHE DATE     TTC
 176       10/27/93       K8         0006    00556.00    00/00/00       B00
 176       09/21/93       K8         0007    00638.00    PRIOR SUSPENSE

END




PAGE 004
TO: LHS3   FROM: CLETS                          12/09/93  03:12:32
IV


DATE: 12/09/93 TIME: 03:11
REG VALID FROM: 12/16/90 TO 12/16/91
LIC#:■■■■■■2 YRMD:84 MAKE:CHEV BTM :PM VIN :10■■■■■■■■■■■■■2
R/O :■■■■S ■■■■■A J■■■■■■, ■■■■ W ■■■■■■ ST CITY:HANFORD C.C.:16
ZIP#:93230
SOLD:00/00/84 RCID:07/05/91 OCID:07/17/91 LOCD:3
TYPE:11 POWR:G VEH :17 BODY:J CLAS:CQ
REC STATUS:
07/05/91 VR INSPECTION EXEMPTION


CLEARANCE INFORMATION RECORDS
OFFICE    WORK DATE     TECH/ID     SEQ #     VALUE      FICHE DATE     TTC
 626       01/12/89       14         0054    00150.00    00/00/00       B00
 626       12/06/89       11         0003    00092.00    00/00/00       I05
 626       12/11/90       10         0047    00080.00    00/00/00       I05
 657       06/28/91       10         0032    00009.00    00/00/00       RIP
 657       06/20/91       09         0043    00009.00    PRIOR SUSPENSE
 657       07/05/91       10         0066    00009.00    00/00/00       F00
 657       06/28/91       10         0032    00009.00    PRIOR SUSPENSE
002 TOTAL RECORDS
```

(16)

PAGE 005

MORE

DATE: 12/09/93 TIME: 03:11
REG VALID FROM: 06/20/93 TO 06/20/94
LIC#:[redacted]2 YRMD:84 MAKE:CHEV BTM :PM VIN :[redacted]
R/O :[redacted]Z A[redacted]D M[redacted]D, [redacted]5 W [redacted] ST CITY:HANFORD C.C.:16
ZIP#:93230
RCID:10/27/93 OCID:11/07/93 LOCD:5
TYPE:11 POWR:G VEH :13 BODY:J CLAS:BV *-YR:91
REC STATUS:
10/27/93 VR INSPECTION EXEMPTION
10/27/93 [illegible] LIC [redacted]

[illegible] INFORMATION RECORDS

OFFICE	WORK DATE	TECH/ID	SEQ #	VALUE	FICHE DATE	TTC
176	10/27/93	K8	0006	00556.00	00/00/00	800
176	09/21/93	K8	0007	00638.00	PRIOR SUSPENSE	

PAGE 006
END

093 [redacted]

```
PAGE 001  12/09/93  03:15:32 LHSP PRINT REQUESTED BY TERMINAL LHS3
TO: LHS3  FROM: CLETS                    12/09/93  03:15:27
UA
SVS ENTRY
IMPOUNDED VEHICLE
LIC/[redacted]2 84 CHEV TK LL BLU/WHI VIN/[redacted]2
LIS/CA LIY/94 LIT/TK
ORI/CA0190022 OCA/930927210 DOT/120893 FCN/2329334300623
MIS/SIERRA TOW 818 707 2197 AUTHY 22655 5A2VC
ENT/ON CALIF FILE ONLY
```

```
PAGE 001  12/09/93  03:16:01 LHSP PRINT REQUESTED BY TERMINAL LHS3
TO: LHS3  FROM: CLETS                    12/09/93  03:15:49
IV

DATE: 12/09/93 TIME: 03:14
REG VALID FROM: 06/20/93 TO 06/20/94
LIC#:3[redacted]D:84 MAKE:CHEV BTM :PM VIN :[redacted]
R/O :[redacted] W [redacted] ST CITY:HANFORD C.C.:16
ZIP#:93230
RCID:10/27/93 OCID:11/07/93 LOCD:5
TYPE:11 POWR:G VEH :13 BODY:J CLAS:BV *-YR:91
REC STATUS:
10/27/93 VR INSPECTION EXEMPTION
10/27/93 PREV LIC [redacted]

CLEARANCE INFORMATION RECORDS
OFFICE   WORK DATE    TECH/ID   SEQ #    VALUE     FICHE DATE    TTC
 176      10/27/93      K8       0006   00556.00    00/00/00     B00
 176      09/21/93      K8       0007   00638.00    PRIOR SUSPENSE

END
```

04-

```
GE 002
  LHS3  FROM: CLETS                          12/09/93  03:15:50

 CA0190022.LIC/ LIS/C

QUIRY MATCH ON LIC/3
POUNDED VEHICLE
C/ 84 CHEV TK LL BLU/WHI VIN/
S/CA LIY/94 LIT/TK
I/CA0190022 OCA/930927210 DOT/120893 FCN/2329334300623
S/SIERRA TOW 818 707 2197 AUTHY 22655 5A2VC
T/ON CALIF FILE ONLY
MEDIATELY CONFIRM WITH ORI/CA0190022 LASD LOST HILLS MNE/LJU
LEPHONE 818 878-1808
```

\ RED

COUNTY OF LOS ANGELES - SHERIFF'S DEPARTMENT - SUPPLEMENTARY REPORT

DATE DECEMBER 14, 1993 **FILE NO.** 093-[redacted]

C- MURDER - 187 P.C. **Action Taken** ACTIVE/INVESTIGATION MADE/EVIDENCE HELD/ CC#93-11360

V- (SEE BELOW)

D- 12-08-93 (WEDNESDAY) AT 1346 HOURS

L- DECKER CANYON ROAD, 1.2 MILES NORTH OF PACIFIC COAST HIGHWAY, MALIBU

S- UNKNOWN

VICTIM:

[redacted], [redacted] MH/35 DOB: 01-17-58
[redacted] AVENUE
OXNARD, CA
CII #A08006042, FBI #82515FA8, CDL #C1581401, POB: MEXICO

EVIDENCE HELD:

Item #1 - Four expended .25 caliber brass shell casings, head stamped "R-P .25 Auto", found on the floor board of the victim's vehicle.

Item #2 - One expended copper bullet found on the floor of the victim's vehicle.

Item #3 - Four expended copper bullets recovered from the victim's body on 12-10-93 during an autopsy by Dr. Riley.

****

On 12-08-93 at 1940 hours, Investigators responded to the location to investigate the shooting death of Victim [redacted].

Investigators contacted Deputy Mike [redacted] and his partner Deputy Joe [redacted]s, P.M. Unit 104, Lost Hills Station. Deputy [redacted] stated at approximately 1346 hours on Wednesday, 12-08-93, the victim was found dead in a parked pick-up truck at the location. Further investigation indicated that the victim had been shot multiple time with a small caliber weapon. The deputies cordoned off the crime scene and talked to possible witnesses in the area. The

victim's vehicle, a 1984 Chevrolet pick-up truck, blue and white in color, with a blue and white camper shell, License #[redacted]2, is registered to the victim's brother, [redacted]o, at [redacted] [redacted] Street, Hanford, California.

Investigators observed the crime scene to be an unpaved dirt turn-out on the side of Decker Canyon Road, 1.2 miles north of Pacific Coast Highway. Decker Canyon Road is a winding mountainous road in extremely hilly terrain. This particular turn-out has a graded cut-out going from the roadway beneath the turn-out, into the mountain side. The victim's vehicle was parked pointed outward in this cut-out, as if it had been backed in. Investigators observed the driver's door window to be rolled down and the passenger's door window to be rolled up. The ignition keys were in the ignition. The ignition was turned off and the transmission was in park. The passenger door was open. Investigators observed five cassette tapes with Mexican labels, laying on the front seat. There was one plastic bottle of Pennzoil Motor Oil on the front seat.

There was one bottle of Hansen's Lemonade laying on the front seat that appeared to be partially drank. Investigators turned the ignition on and the vehicle started immediately indicating that the battery was in good condition. The radio was turned on to 1020 AM with the volume on a low setting. This radio station is a Spanish speaking station. Investigators retrieved Evidence Held Item #1, shell casings, from the floor board of the vehicle. Three shell casings and the expended bullet were on the right front floor board, laying in some blood spots. One expended shell casing was retrieved from the interior driver's door ledge, on the floor, to the left of the driver's seat.

At the time of Investigators arrival, Coroner's Investigator [redacted] had already responded to the location and removed the victim's body from the truck floor board and laid him out on the ground near the truck. The original position of the victim's body had been laying on his left side with his head touching the right passenger door. His feet were almost against the left driver's door. His entire body was off of the seat and laying in front of the seat on the floor board. Investigators observed the victim to be a male Hispanic with thick black hair and a thick mustache. He was wearing a brown leather jacket with a snap up front over a blue and white flannel shirt. He was also wearing black Levis with a lizard or snake skin belt and brown Tony Lama cowboy boots. There were several Mexican coins in the victim's pockets.

Investigators also observed two vehicle license plates #[redacted] labeled "JAL.MEX". Initial observations of the victim at the scene indicated that he had been shot several times in the left shoulder area with a small caliber weapon. Coroner Investigator [redacted] administered Coroner GSR Kit #A2346 to the victim's hands at

1925 hours. The victim's vehicle was impounded at Sierra Tow, 2326 Townsgate Road, West Lake Village, (818) 707-2197. During a search of the victim's vehicle, Investigators came across a white envelope with an address of [redacted] Drive, Oxnard, 93030.

At 2205 hours, Investigators responded to the address in Oxnard and contacted [redacted]L, [redacted]O [redacted], MH/27, ([redacted]5) [redacted]3-[redacted]0. Witness [redacted] was asked if he knew anyone by the name of [redacted] [redacted]z (the registered owner of the truck). Mr. [redacted] responded that he did not know [redacted]o [redacted], but he was acquainted with a [redacted]. In explaining this association, Mr. [redacted] stated [redacted] had been his connection some time ago for large quantities of cocaine which Mr. [redacted] was subsequently arrested, in possession of, by San Luis Obispo Narcotics Investigators. In 1990, Mr. [redacted] was convicted of possession of "narcotics for sale" and stated that he had done two years in State Prison. Upon his release from State Prison in May of 1992, he indicated that [redacted] contacted him and stated that Mr. [redacted] owed him in excess of $90,000.00.

Mr. [redacted] stated that [redacted] was at his house the previous night demanding payment and stated that he would return tonight and burn down his (Mr. [redacted]'s) house if he (Mr. [redacted]) could not provide any funds. Mr. [redacted] stated that he and his family had been receiving threats for numerous months from Mr. [redacted] in regards to this past debt. Mr. [redacted] had his brother, [redacted], MH/29, DOB: 02-16-64, come over to his house, this evening, to help protect his family if Mr. [redacted]z and his associates should return. Investigators asked Mr. [redacted] where he was during the A.M. hours, this date, and he indicated that he and his brother, along with [redacted]y [redacted], [redacted] (his brother-in-law), and his father [redacted] were working at the [redacted] Motel, in Malibu.

Mr. [redacted] said he arrived on the job at approximately 0830 hours and left at 1700 hours. Mr. [redacted] works for his father's company which is [redacted], Oxnard, ([redacted]) [redacted]-2[redacted], ([redacted]) [redacted]-[redacted]. He stated on the previous evening when [redacted]z made the threats to he and his family, he ([redacted]) was accompanied by another male Hispanic who he described as 5' 8", skinny, 28 to 30 years old, with straight hair combed back, and wearing a jacket. He stated [redacted] was wearing a brown leather jacket and driving a blue and white Chevrolet pick-up truck with a camper shell. Mr. [redacted] stated in 1992 he gave [redacted] a 1984 VW, convertible, a spa and a large TV set as partial payment on his drug debt. Mr. [redacted] stated [redacted] knows his entire family and has worked on occasion for his father and his uncle, [redacted] [redacted]. All the work that [redacted] did for Mr. [redacted]'s uncle and father was conducted in the Malibu area.

On 12-09-93 at 0930 hours, Investigators contacted ████ ████s parole officer ████a ████, (███) ████1. She indicated that Mr. ████ had called her on the day of the murder at approximately 0800 to 0900 hours just to check in. She said he is on minimum supervision and has had a clean record since being paroled in 1992. During the phone conversation he sounded as if he wanted to talk about something and she made an appointment for an interview on Friday, 12-10-93. She further revealed that ████ ████, true name ████ ████ ████, MW/30, DOB: 07-08-63, was a crime partner of Mr. ████ during the 1990 cocaine arrest in San Luis Obispo.

Other individuals involved in that arrest were ████ ████ ████n, MB/28, DOB: 09-11-65, ████ ████a, MH/35, DOB: 09-23-58, and ████ ████n ████e, FW/26, DOB: 02-13-67. This investigation and arrest was conducted by the Narcotics Task Force of San Luis Obispo County and involved the confiscation of ap- [illegible] arrest indicated that ████ ████ [illegible] the case.

On 12-09-93, Investigators responded to the ████ ████ Motel on Pacific Coast Highway to interview co-workers of Mr. ████.

Investigators contacted ████ ████ ████, MW/30, DOB: 07-08-63, ████ ████ "E" Street, Oxnard, (███) ████. Mr. ████n stated in 1990 he was arrested with Mr. ████ in San Luis Obispo for the possession of several kilos of cocaine. He stated on 12-08-93 he was working at the location with Mr. ████ repairing a septic tank. He said that he did not get to work until approximately 1200 hours because he had picked up one of the work trucks in Oxnard and taken it to ████ Tires, in Oxnard, to have several tires changed. He stated he then drove to the Malibu site arriving sometime around 1200 hours. He said when he arrived everyone else was there.

Investigators then contacted ████ ████D, ████ Malibu Road, Malibu, ████, and a work number of ███-████. Mr. ████ is the owner of the ████ ████ Motel. He stated on 12-08-93 he arrived at the motel at approximately 0900 hours and was back and forth between the motel and his residence in Malibu Canyon several times that day. He stated each time he arrived back at the motel Mr. ████ was driving a back hoe and working. He stated he did not remember seeing Mr. ████s brother, ████ ████ or ████ ████, each and every time that he arrived at the location.

On 12-09-93 at 1400 hours, Investigators contacted ████A ████, FW/41, DOB: 01-27-52, ███6 Decker Canyon Road, (███) ███-███6. She stated at approximately 0930 hours on 12-08-93 she was driving down Decker Canyon Road and upon approaching the location,

observed the victim standing outside his blue and white pick-up truck, near the driver's door. At the time, the pick-up truck was pointed up hill blocking the road. She further observed a second vehicle behind the pick-up truck which she described as an older brown compact driven by a male White, heavy set, 38 to 40 years old, with thick dark hair. She heard the male in the compact car yell to the victim, "You better get your car out of the way." At this point the witness felt somewhat apprehensive and turned up the mountain in front of the victim's vehicle on Decker Edison Road. As she pulled up the grade she stopped her vehicle and looked down at the victim and the other individual and she yelled down to them, "Do you want me to call someone?"

The second male yelled back at her, "No, we have it under control-." At this point the second male was out of his vehicle and also standing in the middle of the road. She has never seen the victim's vehicle or the compact vehicle in the area before.

On 12-10-93 at 0930 hours, Investigators attended an autopsy at the Los Angeles County Coroner's Office performed by Dr. [redacted]. Dr. [redacted] ascribed the cause of death as multiple gunshot wounds to the torso and a single gunshot wound to the left rear side of the head. All the gunshot wounds appeared to be of small caliber entering the body from the left side and travelling from left to right.

Investigation continuing with further reports to follow.

BY: SERGEANT [redacted] K [redacted], #[redacted]
INVESTIGATOR M[redacted] [redacted], #0[redacted]
APPROVED BY: LIEUTENANT [redacted]
HOMICIDE BUREAU - DETECTIVE DIVISION

[redacted]/WPII

(24)

\ RED

COUNTY OF LOS ANGELES - SHERIFF'S DEPARTMENT - SUPPLEMENTARY REPORT

DATE MAY 10, 1994 FILE NO. 093-[redacted]

C- MURDER - 187 P.C. Action Taken ACTIVE/ADDITIONAL INFORMATION

V- [redacted], [redacted] [redacted]/36, DOB: 01-17-58

D- 12-08-93 AT 1346 HOURS

L- DECKER CANYON 1.2 MILES NORTH OF PACIFIC COAST HIGHWAY

S-

On 05-09-94, Investigators responded to 416 East Poplar Street Oxnard, to interview Witness [redacted] who is the registered owner of the murder weapon in this case.

Investigators advised [redacted] why he was being interviewed and he became very nervous and visibly shaken. He first stated he sold his .25 caliber Beretta at a gun show sometime in late 1990 to a male who he could not describe. Investigators provided the witness with a xeroed copy of Section 32 of the Penal Code and asked him to read it. After reading the Penal Code Section the witness became very quiet and finally stated that shortly after he recovered his Beretta .25 caliber handgun from Oxnard Police Department, (it had been taken for safe keeping during a 1990 arrest involving his brother Renato) he gave the gun to his brother [redacted] for home protection.

He stated that he knows the [redacted] family because they used to live in the same neighborhood. He also stated that he knows the [redacted] brothers because they used to live on the same street. The witness stated that to his knowledge his brother [redacted] still owns the .25 caliber Beretta. [redacted] advised Investigators that his brother [redacted] worked at the Point Magu Naval Weapons station.

Investigators responded to Point Magu and were advised that [redacted] [redacted] is a private contractor on the naval base and that he was at lunch. Upon leaving the Naval Station we observed [redacted] [redacted] and his mother parked in a parking lot just off of the naval station grounds talking to a male adult. Investigators approached the group and learned that [redacted] and his mother were at the location to discuss the incident with [redacted].

Investigators then interviewed [redacted] MH/35, DOB: 12-23-59, [redacted] [redacted] Street, Pomona, 90626-7912. Witness [redacted]

stated that sometime after Thanksgiving of 1993 his brother [redacted] told him that he needed protection. He said that he knew that his brother [redacted] owed some people money from his cocaine arrest and Renato asked if he could borrow the .25 caliber Beretta. Witness [redacted] stated he gave the Beretta, .25 caliber handgun to his brother [redacted] unloaded with about 8 loose bullets. He said since that time he has not discussed the weapon with [redacted] and to his knowledge [redacted] should know where the weapon is.

Investigators then responded to the Ventura County jail to interview Witness [redacted] [redacted] **MH/35, DOB: 09-23-59.** Witness [redacted] [redacted] is in custody at the Ventura County jail for a parole violation. Investigators contacted Witness [redacted] [redacted] in a interview room and noted that the witness was very uncooperative. Investigators advised the witness of the circumstances surrounding their interview with him and he stated, "I haven't had a gun since 1989 because I'm on parole and I can't have a gun." Investigators advised the witness that his brother [redacted] had made a statement indicating that he ([redacted]) should know the whereabouts of the .25 caliber handgun. [redacted] replied that he could not say that [redacted] lied to Investigators about giving him a gun but he denied ever having a gun.

He also stated that he has never received any threats from anyone. Investigators showed the witness a photograph of the victim and he stated that he had never seen the victim before. The witness stated, "I just got out of prison and its you against me." Investigators asked the witness if he would take a polygraph test and he refused stating that he was not going to make our job any easier. The witness then stated, "Take your case to the D.A. it's your job, I won't help you do your job, I want an attorney." The interview was then terminated at this time.

BY: SERGEANT R[redacted] [redacted]N, #[redacted]
INVESTIGATOR M[redacted]L [redacted], #[redacted]
APPROVED BY: A/LIEUTENANT C[redacted] [redacted]R
HOMICIDE BUREAU - DETECTIVE DIVISION

[redacted]/I.S.

\ RED

COUNTY OF LOS ANGELES - SHERIFF'S DEPARTMENT - SUPPLEMENTARY REPORT

DATE MAY 10, 1994 FILE NO. 093-[redacted]1

C- MURDER - 187 P.C. Action Taken ACTIVE/ADDITIONAL INFORMATION

V- [redacted], [redacted] [redacted]S MH/35

D-

L-

S-

INVESTIGATION SUMMARY AS OF MAY 10, 1994

On Wednesday, 12-08-93, the victim was found dead in a pick-up truck parked in a road side turn-out on Decker Canyon Road in Malibu. The victim had been shot five times in the head and upper torso with a .25 caliber pistol, and was found lying face down on the floorboard of the truck. The vehicle was registered to his brother, [redacted] [redacted] [redacted], with a Hanford California address. Reportedly the brother was in Mexico while the victim was using the truck. A letter dated 12-06-93, was found in the truck addressed to the resident at [redacted] [redacted] [redacted] in Oxnard.

Investigators responded to the [redacted] [redacted] address during the late hours of 12-08-93 and contacted [redacted] [redacted] MH/27. [redacted] admitted to knowing the victim and further to owing him in an excess of $60,000 dollars for cocaine that had been seized during a police investigation in San Luis Obipso County in 1990. [redacted] related that the victim had been to the [redacted]'s home on 12-07-93 and had personally threatened [redacted] and his family with bodily harm if [redacted] could not come up with $50,000 dollars for the drug debt. Reportedly the victim stated that he would come back on the evening of 12-08-93, to collect his money and if [redacted] could not pay the debt the victim would burn the [redacted]'s residence down.

During subsequent interviews [redacted] stated that the victim was a cocaine mule from Mexico and had provided cocaine to [redacted] on various occasions prior to the 1990 arrest. San Luis Obipso authorities confirmed that [redacted] had been arrested in a multi-kilo cocaine investigation in 1990 along with a [redacted] [redacted], [redacted] [redacted], and [redacted] [redacted]. [redacted] also stated that a close friend by the name of [redacted] [redacted], owed the victim

MAY 10, 1994 -2- 093-[redacted]

$50,000 dollars for cocaine. [redacted] also had been receiving threats from the victim.

Fingerprint examination of the victim's vehicle revealed a fingerprint belonging to [redacted] on the left side cab of the victim's truck. [redacted] is the younger brother of [redacted]o. The [redacted] were contacted by Investigators and confirmed that they had received threats from the victim and his associates and that [redacted] did in fact owe [redacted] $90,000 dollars. [redacted] admitted to running off two male Hipanics from the family home sometime in December of 1993. These individuals were at the [redacted] residence trying to locate [redacted] and making threats to the [redacted] family. [redacted]o does not remember the victim, the victim's truck, or touching the victim's truck.

Shell casings and bullets at the crime scene were positively matched to a .25 caliber Beretta pistol which was seized in a narcotics raid by Oxnard Police Detectives on 01-11-94. This weapon was registered to [redacted], the younger brother of [redacted]. Investigators contacted [redacted] who stated that he was in fact the owner of the .25 caliber Beretta. Sometime in late 1990 he gave the gun to his older brother, [redacted], who lived in Pomona. Investigators contacted [redacted] at his place of employment at the Point Mugu Naval Station. [redacted] stated that he did have the gun in question from late 1990 until shortly after Thanksgiving of 1993. At that time his brother [redacted] asked him for the weapon and told him that he was being threatened by some very bad people and he needed the gun for protection.

Investigators next contacted [redacted]a at the Ventura County Jail where he is in custody for drunk driving and parole violation. [redacted] was confronted with the facts of this case to this point and he denied any knowledge of the handgun indicating that he was on parole and has not had a handgun since 1989. He was shown pictures of the victim and the victim's truck and he stated he did not know the victim and has never seen him or his truck before. [redacted] refused to take a lie detector test regarding his possession of this handgun and stated that he would not aid Investigators in this investigation in any way.

Case to remain active investigation to follow.

BY: SERGEANT P[redacted], #[redacted]
INVESTIGATOR M[redacted], #[redacted]
APPROVED BY: A/LIEUTENANT [redacted]
HOMICIDE BUREAU - DETECTIVE DIVISION

[redacted]/I.S.

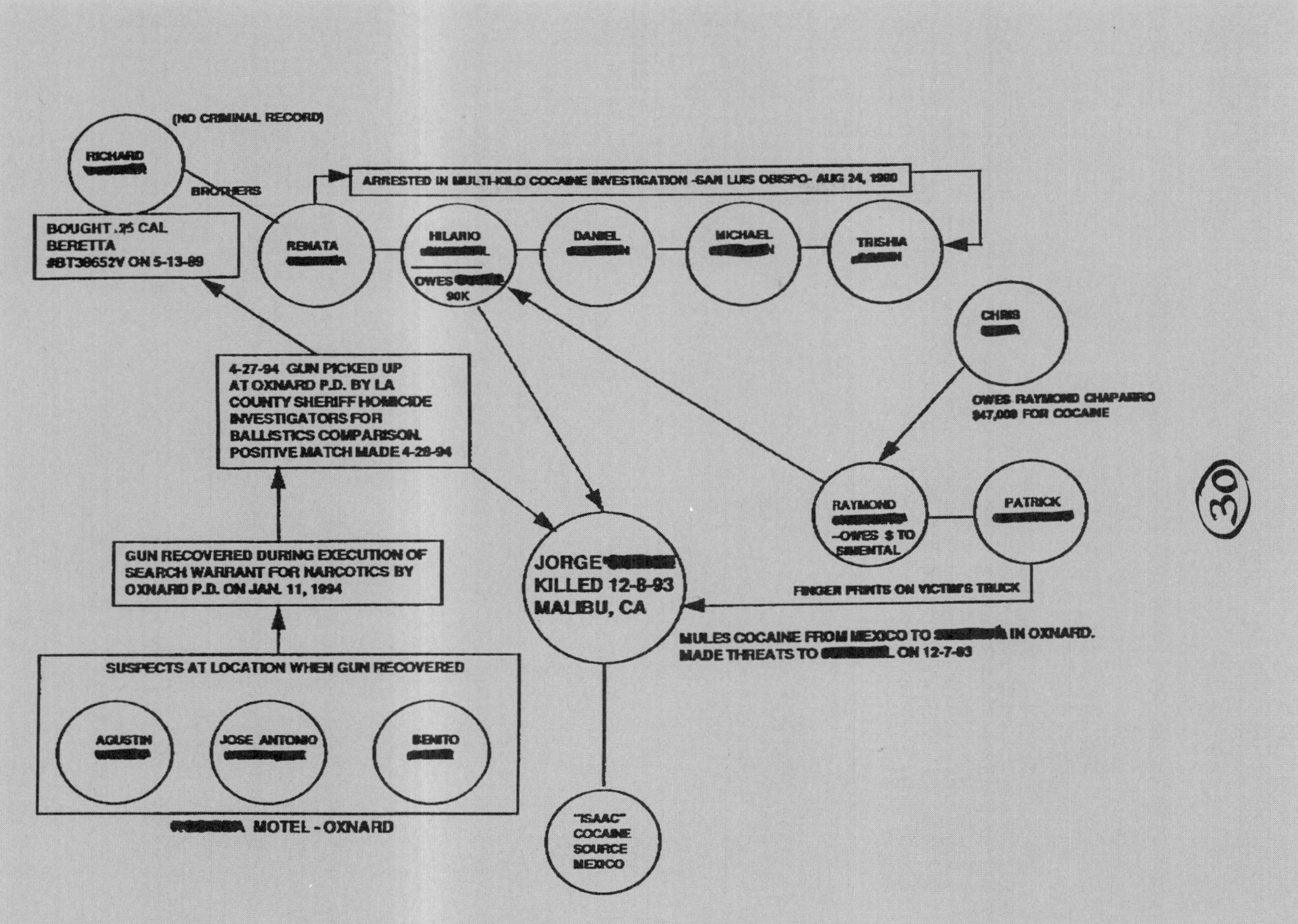
(NO CRIMINAL RECORD)
RICHARD
BROTHERS
BOUGHT .25 CAL
BERETTA
#BT38652V ON 5-13-89
ARRESTED IN MULTI-KILO COCAINE INVESTIGATION -SAN LUIS OBISPO- AUG 24, 1990
RENATA
HILARIO
OWES
90K
DANIEL
MICHAEL
TRISHIA
CHRIS
OWES RAYMOND CHAPARRO
$47,000 FOR COCAINE
4-27-94 GUN PICKED UP
AT OXNARD P.D. BY LA
COUNTY SHERIFF HOMICIDE
INVESTIGATORS FOR
BALLISTICS COMPARISON.
POSITIVE MATCH MADE 4-28-94
RAYMOND
-OWES $ TO
SIMENTAL
PATRICK
GUN RECOVERED DURING EXECUTION OF
SEARCH WARRANT FOR NARCOTICS BY
OXNARD P.D. ON JAN. 11, 1994
JORGE
KILLED 12-8-93
MALIBU, CA
FINGER PRINTS ON VICTIM'S TRUCK
MULES COCAINE FROM MEXICO TO IN OXNARD.
MADE THREATS TO ON 12-7-93
SUSPECTS AT LOCATION WHEN GUN RECOVERED
AGUSTIN
JOSE ANTONIO
BENITO
MOTEL - OXNARD
"ISAAC"
COCAINE
SOURCE
MEXICO
30

\ RED

COUNTY OF LOS ANGELES - SHERIFF'S DEPARTMENT - SUPPLEMENTARY REPORT

DATE MAY 12, 1994 **FILE NO.** 093-

C- MURDER - 187 P.C. **Action Taken** ACTIVE/INVESTIGATION MADE/EVIDENCE HELD/ CC#93-11360

V- , **JORGE** **MH/36** DOB: 01-17-58

D- 12-08-93 (WEDNESDAY) AT 1346 HOURS

L- DECKER CANYON ROAD 1.2 MILES NORTH OF PACIFIC COAST HIGHWAY, MALIBU

S-

EVIDENCE HELD:

Item #1 - One Beretta, .25 caliber pistol, model 950, blue steel, serial #BT38652V.

Item #2 - Two ammunition magazines for the above Beretta pistol and one box of .25 caliber "ACP" ammunition.

****

On 04-27-94, Investigators met with Detective Ron from the Oxnard Police Department and discussed the circumstances surrounding this investigation.

Investigators advised Detective that they were investigating the murder of Victim Jorge which occurred on December 8, 1993, on Decker Canyon Road, Malibu. Investigation revealed Victim was possibly a "narcotics mule" from Mexico who supplied Hilario and several associates in Oxnard with cocaine. Detective checked evidence records at Oxnard Police Department for any .25 caliber pistols that had been confiscated by that agency after December 8, 1993. Computer records revealed that the Evidence Held Beretta pistol was confiscated by Oxnard Police Department Narcotic Investigators on January 11, 1994, at the Motel, Room #11, Saviers Road, Oxnard. The gun was recovered during a search warrant executed at that location involving the arrests of , MH/DOB: 11-21-64, AKA: "Benito ", Augustine , MH/DOB: 07-29-65 and 02-22-65, and Jose , MH/DOB: 09-11-59.

Examination of ballistics evidence from the murder scene compared to the Evidence Held pistol by Deputy , from the

Sheriff's Crime Lab on 04-28-94, was a positive match. State computer records reflected that the registered owner of this weapon is ███ ███an ███a, MH/DOB: 04-29-68, ███ ███t ███r ███t, Oxnard. Mr. ███ purchased the Beretta on May 13, 1989. At this point it is unknown if Mr. ███ has any connection with the suspects arrested at the ███a Motel. Investigation has revealed, however, that Mr. ███ is the brother of Renato ███, a known associate of Hilario ███ ███. Hilario ███ and Renato ███a were arrested in a multi-kilo cocaine investigation in San Luis Obispo County in 1990.

Reportedly the seized cocaine was provided to ███ by Victim Jorge ███. ███ claimed that since the cocaine provided by ███z was seized during the San Luis Obispo arrest, Victim ███z and his source, "Isaac", MH/27, unknown address in Mexico, were never reimbursed for the seized cocaine. ███ also stated Victim ███z and another male associate came to his Oxnard residence on 12-07-93 demanding money in payment for the seized cocaine. ███z reportedly told ███l that he would return on the evening of 12-08-93 (day of ███ murder) and would burn ███'s house down if ███l did not pay him $50,000. ███z was murdered during the morning or early afternoon of 12-08-93 with a gun subsequently found to be registered to Richard ███. Investigation also revealed a fingerprint on the left side of the victim's truck which was identified as belonging to Patrick ███, MH/DOB: 02-14-70, ███ ███ ███, Oxnard.

At 1300 hours on 04-27-94, Investigators responded to the ███ ███ address and contacted **RAYMOND** ███ ███, MH/DOB: 04-08-67, (███) ███-███ and (███) ███-███. Raymond admitted to selling cocaine in the past and serving "time" in State prison for narcotic sales. He said he was released from prison in 1992 and his cocaine source was a close associate by the name of Hilario ███, AKA: "Lalo". He said Hilario's connection in Mexico was a individual by the name of "Isaac" MH/28 or 29 years old. Isaac is based in an unknown location in Mexico and reportedly Victim Jorge ███ was his "mule" to transport cocaine from Mexico to the Oxnard area. Raymond said Gomez would deliver numerous kilos to "Lalo's" residence in Oxnard and leave them on the garage floor. Raymond said he owed ███ 90,000.00 dollars for cocaine that had been seized in two different investigations. Forty-seven thousand dollars of this narcotics is owed to Raymond ███ by an individual by the name of Chris ███, MH/21 or 22 years old.

Raymond said when he got out of State prison and returned home, the victim and several associates began making threats to the ███ family and to Raymond personally. This was done in an effort to recover money owed for the narcotics which had been seized. Raymond said he last saw the victim in February or March of 1993 and at that time he gave him $2,000.00, a Kawasaki motorcycle belonging to Chris ███, and all of ███ wife's

jewelry. Raymond said this property was loaded into a VW Van which broke down at the [redacted] residence. He said Chris [redacted] moved to the Philippine Islands to escape threats from Victim [redacted] and his associates. Raymond said the property given to the victim, in February or March, "bought" him six months of time to raise more money. [redacted] said he would return around August or September for payment. Raymond has not seen [redacted] or his associates since. Raymond said he is a very close associate of Hilario [redacted] and that [redacted] advised him that the victim had been murdered. Raymond said he knew the victim by the name "Hoppo".

Investigators next interviewed **PATRICK** [redacted], MH/DOB: 02-14-70, [redacted], Oxnard. Patrick said he is a frequent drug user and drinks alcohol almost on a daily basis. He said on at least two occasions male Hispanics, who were Spanish speaking, have been to the [redacted] residence asking for his brother Raymond and threatening to harm the family if Raymond didn't pay the money owed for the seized cocaine. He said two males, nfd., came to the house one night in December about 2200 hours wanting his brother Raymond. Raymond wasn't home and Patrick closed the door of the residence and went outside on the front lawn with the two men. Patrick said he was drinking and using narcotics that night and he could not recognize a picture of the victim or the victim's truck. Patrick said he armed himself with a kitchen knife and told these two males to leave his residence and take their business up with Raymond.

Patrick said he walked them to the curb and does not remember touching their vehicle. He does not remember if they were driving a truck, van, or a car. Patrick was confronted with the fact that his fingerprints had been found on the victim's truck at the murder scene. He could not explain why his fingerprints were on the truck. Patrick could not recognize pictures of the victim or the victim's brother, Adolfo [redacted], MH/DOB: 06-26-55, the registered owner of the truck, which the victim was found in.

Investigation continuing with further reports to follow.

BY: SERGEANT P[redacted], #[redacted]
INVESTIGATOR M[redacted], #[redacted]
APPROVED BY: A/LIEUTENANT [redacted]
HOMICIDE BUREAU - DETECTIVE DIVISION

[redacted]/WPII

LOS ANGELES COUNTY SHERIFF'S DEPARTMENT
SCIENTIFIC SERVICES BUREAU
FIREARMS IDENTIFICATION SECTION

PAGE 1 of 1

REC'D FROM		FILE	
[redacted] / [redacted] - Homicide Bureau		093-[redacted]	
DATE December 1, 1993	C- 187 P.C.	RECEIPT H392545	
SUSPECT. ---		VICTIM [redacted], Jorge	

GRC	CALIBER	NO. L&G	TWIST	LAND IMP. WIDTH	GROOVE IMP. WIDTH
	25 auto	6	R	.038	.090

ITEM	#93-11360 (1 of 4)	#93-11360 (2 of 4)	#93011360 (3 of 4)	#93-11360 (4 of4)
TYPE	Full metal jacket	FMJ	FMJ	FMJ
WEIGHT	50.3 grains	50.2 grains	49.9 grains	49.7 grains
MAKE	Unknown	Unknown	Unknown	Unknown
PERCENTAGE MUTILATION	---	---	---	---
CONTAMINATION	---	---	---	---
MARKS OF VALUE FOR COMPARISON	Yes	Yes	Yes	Yes

OTHER EVIDENCE - OPINIONS - COMMENTS

EVIDENCE

Item #1, 2, 4 and 5 - Four envelopes each containing one expended 25 auto caliber cartridge case (RP)

Item #3 - One envelope containing one expended full metal jacket bullet (Wt. = 49.9 grains)

OPINION

The five expended bullets (items #93-11360 (1 of 4) - (4 of 4) and #3) were all fired in the same firearm. Firearms known to have the same general rifling characteristics include pistols manufactured by Beretta, Browning, RG and Titan.

The four expended 25 auto caliber cartridge cases (items #1, 2, 4 and 5) were all fired in the same firearm.

FIREARMS EXAMINER	SIGNATURE
[redacted]	[signature]
EMPLOYEE NO. [redacted]	DATE December 17, 1993

(34)

LOS ANGELES COUNTY SHERIFF'S DEPARTMENT
SCIENTIFIC SERVICES BUREAU
FIREARMS IDENTIFICATION SECTION

REC'D FROM	FILE
[redacted] - Homicide Bureau	093-[redacted]
DATE: April 28, 1994	RECEIPT: H391886
CAL.: 25 Auto	MAKE: Beretta
MODEL: 950 BS	TYPE: Single action pistol
SERIAL NO.: BT 38652 V	LOCATION: Left side of frame

COUNTRY	CARTRIDGE CAPACITY	BARREL LENGTH	FINISH
U.S.A.	8 + 1	2 1/2"	Blue

ADDITIONAL INFO - CONDITION - OTHER MARKS - BROKEN/MISSING PARTS

Submitted with two magazines, four rounds of 25 Auto caliber ammunition (RP) and one box containing forty four rounds of 25 Auto caliber ammunition (RP).

S/A TRIGGER PULL	IS THIS NORMAL	D/A TRIGGER PULL	IS THIS NORMAL	FIRED SINCE LAST CLEANING
8 Lbs.	Yes	-----	-----	Yes

NO. TIMES TEST FIRED	DID FIREARM FUNCTION NORMALLY DURING TEST FIRING - IF NO, EXPLAIN
2	Yes

GRC	CALIBER	NO. L&G	TWIST	LAND IMP. WIDTH	GROOVE IMP. WIDTH
	25 Auto	6	R	.038	.090

OTHER EVIDENCE WITH FIREARM - OPINIONS - COMMENTS

OPINION

This firearm was compared to evidence previously submitted under laboratory receipt **H392545**. The five expended bullets contained in Items #93-11360 (1 of 4) - (4 of 4) and #3 were all fired from the submitted Beretta pistol. The four expended cartridge cases (Items #1, 2, 4 and 5) were all fired in the submitted Beretta pistol (Serial Number BT 38652 V).

FIREARMS EXAMINER	SIGNATURE
[redacted]	[redacted]
EMPLOYEE NO.: 248131	DATE: May 2, 1994

35

LOS ANGELES COUNTY DISTRICT ATTORNEY

CHARGE EVALUATION WORKSHEET

(T055)

☐ Further investigation requested.
☐ Probation Violation in lieu of filed.
☒ Prosecution declined.

DA CASE NO. R743361

POLICE CASE NO. (DR OR URN NO.) 093 [redacted]

Page 1 of 1

17. Date (Mo.-Day-Year) 08-29-94

DA OFFICE CODE MAL

SUSPECT DATA

SUSP NO	SUSPECT NAME (LAST-FIRST-MIDDLE)	19. BOOKING NO.	20. CHARGES CODE	SECTION	SUB SECTION	REASON CODES (CIRCLE ONE/COUNT)
1	[redacted], RENALTO	NIC	P	187		A (B) C D E F G / H I J K L M N
						A B C D E F G / H I J K L M N
2						A B C D E F G / H I J K L M N
						A B C D E F G / H I J K L M N
3						A B C D E F G / H I J K L M N
						A B C D E F G / H I J K L M N
4						A B C D E F G / H I J K L M N
						A B C D E F G / H I J K L M N

DOJ REASON CODES — FOR USE ON THIS FORM AND JUS-8715

A. Lack of Corpus
B. Lack of Sufficient Evidence
C. Inadmissable Search & Seizure
D. Victim Unavailable/Declines to Testify
E. Witness Unavailable/Declines to Testify
F. Combined with Other Counts/Cases
G. Interest of Justice
H. Other - Indicate the Reason in "Remarks" Section
I. Referred to non-California Jurisdiction
J. Deferred for Revocation of Parole
K. Further Investigation
L. Prosecutor Prefiling Deferral

L.A. COUNTY D.A. REASON CODES — NOT FOR USE ON JUS-8715

M. Probation Violation in lieu of filed.
N. Referred to C.A. for Misdemeanor Consideration.

DESCRIPTION

Victim was involved in narco importation in association w/suspect + others. Arrests resulted in seizure of ± $100,000 of narcotics + state prison commitments. Victim + associates were threatening suspect + suspect's co-arrestees in prior narco case to induce them to make good on lost to seizure narcotics. Suspect was given murder weapon by suspect's brother much prior to murder — Suspect denies this. No other evidence to connect suspect to crime. Prosecution declined - insufficient ev. to convict.

PROMIS CHECK COMPLETE

IRA REINER District Attorney	COMPLAINT DEPUTY (PRINT)	18. DEPUTY CODE	COMPLAINT DEPUTY (SIGNATURE)	REVIEWING DEPUTY
	[redacted]	[redacted]	[redacted]	

In submitting this matter for consideration of a complaint, written reports of substantially all available evidence (except as to the oral information, if any, purporting to have been given by me and which is fully and correctly stated above) have been submitted to the above named Deputy (copies of which are attached hereto) except the following:

The disposition of this matter will be final unless the commanding officer requests reconsideration of the case, stating his reasons on the back of this form.

[redacted signature]

OFFICER

DA-773-H—76R269U—Rev 8/88

(36)

\ RED

COUNTY OF LOS ANGELES - SHERIFF'S DEPARTMENT - SUPPLEMENTARY REPORT

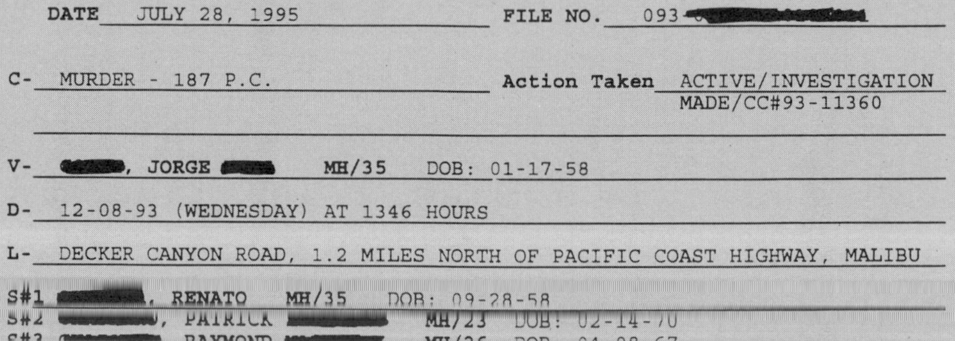

DATE JULY 28, 1995 **FILE NO.** 093-[redacted]

C- MURDER - 187 P.C. **Action Taken** ACTIVE/INVESTIGATION MADE/CC#93-11360

V- [redacted], **JORGE** [redacted] **MH/35** DOB: 01-17-58

D- 12-08-93 (WEDNESDAY) AT 1346 HOURS

L- DECKER CANYON ROAD, 1.2 MILES NORTH OF PACIFIC COAST HIGHWAY, MALIBU

S#1 [redacted], **RENATO** **MH/35** DOB: 09-28-58
S#2 [redacted], PATRICK [redacted] MH/23 DOB: 02-14-70
S#3 [redacted], RAYMOND [redacted] MH/26 DOB: 01-08-67

On 07-18-95, Investigators responded to Lost Hills Station and met with Ventura County Deputy District Attorney [redacted], Ventura County Sheriff's Sergeant [redacted], along with Los Angeles County Deputy District Attorney [redacted], for the purposes of interviewing Witness [redacted], FH/26, DOB: 08-29-66. Witness [redacted] had previously met with Investigators from the Ventura County Sheriff's Department and the Ventura County District Attorney's Office and provided information which indicated that the murder of Jorge [redacted] was perpetrated by her brother-in-law Renato [redacted] and his associates Raymond [redacted] and Patrick [redacted]

Witness Annette [redacted] information indicated that the murder occurred at Magoo Rock in the County of Ventura. She said Patrick [redacted] set the meeting up, Renato [redacted] provided the killing weapon and Patrick [redacted] was the shooter. The three suspects met the victim at Magoo Rock and approached the victim who was seated in his pick-up truck. She said Patrick [redacted] shot the victim several times in the head and upper torso. After the shooting, Renato [redacted] left the crime scene and Patrick [redacted] and his brother, Raymond [redacted] transported the victim in his (victim's) pick-up truck across the Los Angeles County line and dumped the victim in an unknown canyon.

Witness Annette [redacted] said the suspects reportedly felt the case would never be solved because of the high rate of homicides in the Los Angeles County area and the fact that the victim was an illegal alien and a drug dealer. She said the disposal of the murder weapon was delegated to Patrick [redacted] and he was supposed to throw the gun into the ocean.

While interviewing Witness Annette it was learned that she is the estranged wife of Joseph , MH/27, DOB: 04-11-65, the younger brother of Renato Olachea. It was further learned that the majority of her information, regarding this case, is second hand information, which was furnished by her husband Joseph. Reportedly Joseph received this information from his brother Renato and from Raymond . She also obtained some information from Jenny , the mother of Renato, Joseph, Richard and John a, all previously mentioned in this investigation.

According to the witness, Jenny admitted that the victim had been threatening the family through her son Renato. When the decision was made to kill the victim, Jenny gave the plan her blessing. Witness Annette had one on one conversations with Raymond wherein he admitted to planning the murder and planning the disposal of the body in the Los Angeles County area. Reportedly Raymond told Witness Annette that it was Renato's job to obtain the weapon and that he (Raymond) planned the meeting with the victim and assisted his brother (Patrick) in disposing of the body in the Los Angeles County area.

The interview of Witness Annette was tape recorded and will become a permanent part of this file.

The facts of this case will be reviewed and considered by the District Attorney's Office in both Los Angeles County and Ventura County for the purposes of further investigation and possible prosecution.

This investigation is continuing with further reports to follow.

BY: SERGEANT P , #
INVESTIGATOR M , #
APPROVED BY: LIEUTENANT 8-7-95
HOMICIDE BUREAU - DETECTIVE DIVISION

/WPII

The Crime Lab: Preface

By Barry Fisher, Director of Scientific Services Bureau, Los Angeles County Sheriff's Department

Life has a funny way of making twists and turns in your destiny.

It was on May 5, 1969, that I began work as a criminalist at the crime lab in Los Angeles. My Jewish mother's answer to this was, "For this I sent you to college and graduate school? To be a cop?"

Actually, I hadn't had a clue about what I wanted to do after graduating from CCNY (City College of New York) and heading for Purdue University in West Lafayette, Indiana. A Ph.D. in chemistry sounded good, thinking I'd make my name in research. So I went for and got my M.S., ready to take on the world, but marriage has a strange way of not always affording you the path you set out on. Looking back now, I thank the good Lord for that.

It was early 1969 when the California Department of Human Resources called me for an interview, my résumé being everywhere and anywhere. The counselor asked if I ever watched *Perry Mason.* It must be a trick question, I thought. "No, the police department is looking for chemists to work in their crime lab as civilians. It sounds just like *Perry Mason,* doesn't it?" Actually it sounded more like *Quincy,* but he came later. Anyway, I got the job.

I became—and still am—a criminalist, not a criminologist. The latter is kind of a sociologist who studies criminals and the cause of criminality. The former is a physical or natural scientist applying science to criminal investigations.

Criminalistics is heady stuff: Most people rarely have direct experience with the evil side of life. Drugs, rape, abuse, murder, and the like are your steady diet. I love my job, but you have to give up so much. Stated in the most simple form: You lose your innocence. You lose your belief that people are basically good and the few who aren't are society's victims. One day, you realize your world view has shifted. You learn quickly that there are evil people who do contemptible things to other human beings and they look just like you and me. You wonder if perhaps you're living next door to one. You identify with murder victims who sometimes remind you of your family and your kids. At first you become a little paranoid and then, after a while, you become callused to the horror around you. You mentally compartmentalize what you've experienced so as to maintain your own equanimity.

You don't relish talking about what you do because friends and family don't understand. The usual response on learning you're in the Crime Lab is, "Wow! That's fascinating. You must see some interesting cases. Can you tell me about one?"

After a while, I was promoted. First as a supervisor and eventually to Crime Lab Director. Being an administrator is a lot of paperwork and not at all like it was when I was up close and personally working a crime scene, collecting evidence, and going to court to testify as an expert witness. This is not to say that as a manager I don't think I make a difference in helping solve crimes. My job today is making sure that the crime lab machinery is well-oiled.

Budgets are required for supplies, equipment, training, and a myriad of other costly factors that go into making a lab function. My other major role is to know who's who and what's what. Being on a first-name basis with major forensic-science players is important, especially when you need information quickly. The vehicle to accomplish this is professional associations, and being active. Involvement opens doors. When I read about some new, important technique in some scientific journal and I need key information about this new technique, a personal call or e-mail to a colleague in the States or abroad gets fast results.

Having served as president of some major national and international forensic-science organizations enables me to influence forensic science public policy at the state and federal level. I consult for the Justice Department and recommend where research money is spent. I coordinate continuing forensic-science education programs on a national basis and help to set national quality-assurance standards for crime labs around the world, and I teach and mentor those planning a career in forensic sciences.

I know of no other profession with such depth and breadth as forensic science. It is exhilarating when you piece together a complex murder though science and logic. I've felt like a chess grand master jousting with defense attorneys during testimony, although, at times, if forensic science should have proven otherwise, I'm a boost for the defense counsel. Above all, I find it immensely satisfying to be able to influence the criminal justice system, enhance the quality of life, and help see that justice is served. I really love the job!

The Crime Lab (The Silent Witness)

Seldom in a murder case is there an eyewitness. However, in a majority of criminal homicides where the police have not abused or contaminated the crime scene, there is a silent witness to what happened. That silent witness is a piece of physical or trace evidence that the killer left behind that cries to speak out to a criminalist at the scene.

Once all the evidence is collected at the crime scene, it is transported to the Crime Lab. The Crime Lab is where the skills of scientific examination and evaluation are used to resolve social and legal issues that must be presented in a court of law.

Prosecutors today strongly attempt to get a jury to understand not only the job of the forensic scientists who study the physical and trace evidence that links the accused to the murderer, but also to accept the scientific testimony by criminalists as expert witnesses based on their forensic specialty and their study and evaluation of the evidence being presented.

There is an enormity of possible clues that may or may not be discovered by the investigator or members of the CSU. The soil in a tire can tell the investigator where a vehicle has been. The soil found on the sole of the victim's shoe or bare foot can tell the investigator where the victim has been, as can the presence of pollen on the victim. Skin found under a victim's fingernails can lead toward an identification of a suspect and help identify the color of a possible suspect. Dust, lint, and animal hairs from a fur coat all help put the puzzle together.

Police forensic science has ten main disciplines, most of which require a minimum of a bachelor's degree; however, requirements for the position of a criminalist differ in various law enforcement departments as well as in different cities, counties, and states.

The branches of forensic science include:

SEROLOGY: The study of blood, semen, and secretions. This area of criminalistics is extremely important because the serologist can help determine

(1) If the blood found at the scene is human or from an animal.

(2) What is the blood type of the victim and the other type(s) of blood that may be found at the crime scene.

Semen can often determine if the victim has been sexually assaulted as well as offer up a blood type or identification that can be verified by the suspect's DNA.

Secretors can also be a big help in identifying the blood of an assailant and is something that technicians or criminalists look for. All people are not secretors, the ratio being somewhere between sixty percent being secretors and forty percent not. A secretor is an individual whose blood type can be determined from his or her body fluids that may be discovered on a towel, the edge of a cup or drinking glass, on the tip of a cigar or cigarette, or even on the lips, breast, or sexual organ of the victim.

Bloodstain evidence is probably one of the most important aspects in a homicide investigation as it can not only lead to a suspect's blood type but also to the relative position of the victim when assaulted: The blood splatter offers an insight to where the victim was standing, sitting, or lying down, how heavy an object he or she was hit with, and the speed with which the blood flew, and any movements the victim made after the attack. Bloody footprints can identify the direction the suspect took after the attack. The lividity of the victim can reveal the position the victim was in when murdered. (This also could tell the investigator whether or not the victim had been moved after lividity had set in.)

If there is no evidence of blood where a murder is suspected to have taken place, the investigator may call for the use of *luminol*. This chemical will reveal the existence of blood under a black light or quite possibly in a room that is totally dark.

FIREARMS IDENTIFICATION: The examination of the suspected murder weapon and the bullets and shell casings found at the scene. This examination determines if this is the weapon that committed the crime. Firearms Identification differs from Ballistics in that Ballistics primarily concerns itself with the trajectory of the bullet(s) that was fired.

FINGERPRINT ID: The examination of the collected fingerprints, separating those that belong to the victim from all others, which are then run through the system to see if they belong to anyone who has a criminal record or would not normally have been at the scene of the crime. Prints may be sent on to the Federal Bureau of Investigation for a thorough check.

POLYGRAPH: This device is used to determine the truth and validity of a suspect's answers to specific questions.

VOICE PRINTS: These are used to determine if a recorded voice belongs to a possible suspect and to match a voice to a recorded phone conversation, etc.

BALLISTICS: The examination and study of the location and angle of where the actual bullet(s) is located so that the trajectory of the bullet(s) fired can be determined. This can offer some insight into where the shooter was standing, along with the approximate height of the shooter.

QUESTIONED DOCUMENTS: Examination and identification of handwriting, typewriting, printing, ink, and paper, along with all other aspects of any given document, including its maker, date, watermark, and anything that might raise legal questions about the author of and authenticity of a document.

PHYSICAL EVIDENCE TECHNICIAN: This technician examines the physical evidence that can lead an investigator to a suspect and assists the investigator and the prosecutor with legal evidence that will eventually bring about an arrest and formal charges against a suspect. This evidence will later be presented in court once the suspect has been brought to trial.

TRACE EVIDENCE TECHNICIAN: This technician examines all trace evidence, including hair and fibers, glass, paint scrapings, etc.

Forensic scientists in the following areas need a bachelor's degree to not only study and analyze evidence in their area of specialization but also to testify as expert witnesses in court.

FORENSIC ANTHROPOLOGY: The standard techniques of physical anthropology used in identifying skeletal remains and otherwise generally unidentifiable remains.

FORENSIC ENGINEERING: The art and science of applying scientific principles to the investigation, analysis, and reconstruction of physical events.

FORENSIC ODONTOLOGY: The branch of dentistry dealing with dental evidence, identifying teeth or dental work, and presenting those dental findings in the interest of justice.

FORENSIC PATHOLOGY/BIOLOGY: Dealing with the investigation and interpretation of injury or death attributed to violence, as in an accident, a suicide, a criminal homicide, or a death occurring unexpectedly or in an unexplained manner. Much of this is done with the aide of an autopsy. In addition to investigating various body parts, identification of a John Doe victim might be established through birthmarks, scars, tattoos, long-bone x-rays, and dental records.

FORENSIC PSYCHIATRY AND BEHAVIORAL SCIENCE: Dealing with the application of psychiatric theory and practice in legal issues. Today it is used in profiling a type of killer and determining a killer's personality, modus operandi, motive for killing, lifestyle, etc.

FORENSIC TOXICOLOGY: Studies of the harmful effects of such substances as poisons, drugs, alcohol, etc., that are introduced into the human system.

FORENSIC DNA: Tests blood through the DNA process, which, in general, will identify an individual's blood for an almost perfect identification. I say "almost" because, although the theory is that no two people have the same properties in their blood, with the possible exception of identical twins, since the DNA examination process is done at different civilian laboratories, it is often challenged in court.

The Crime Lab is one of the most important tools in the investigation and prosecution of a criminal homicide. The Crime Lab, however, does not set out to prove anyone's guilt or innocence. It functions only to determine the facts based on the evidence found at the crime scene or brought to it by the investigators of a criminal homicide. It does not take sides with either the suspect or law enforcement. Although it is a part of the police department or the sheriff's department, it is there only to present evidence that can be used against a suspect or, in some rare cases, to discover that the evidence found at a crime scene helps clear a suspect of participation in the crime.

CRIME LAB EQUIPMENT FOR CRIME SCENE EXAMINATION

A CSU must be properly equipped when summoned to a crime scene so that they are fully prepared to assist in the crime scene investigation. The following list contains much of the basic equipment used by a CSU:

- Disposable latex gloves
- Clipboard
- Cotton-tipped applicators
- Steel surveyor's tape
- Steel tape measure
- Graph paper
- Rulers (6', 12')
- Flashlight and batteries
- Marking pens
- Coveralls
- Scissors
- Paper towels
- Test tubes and corks
- Rubber bands

- Spatulas
- Adhesive tape
- Magnifying glass
- Cellophane tape
- Rubber bulbs
- Forceps (large and small)
- Disposable pipettes
- Chalk
- Crayons
- Evidence tags
- Evidence sealing tape
- Magnet
- Thumbtacks
- Stapler and staples
- Anti-putrefaction masks
- pH paper
- Paper bags
- Plastic bags
- Cardboard boxes
- Envelopes (all sizes)
- Screwcap glass vials (all sizes)
- Pillboxes
- Metal paint cans with lids

PHOTOGRAPHIC EQUIPMENT
- 35mm camera
- Lenses (normal, wide-angle, micro)
- Film (black-and-white and color)
- Flash and batteries
- Tripod level
- Carrying case
- Video camera (with lights and blank videotape)
- Lens brush
- Lens tissue
- Light meter

FINGERPRINT EQUIPMENT

- Fingerprint brushes
- Lifting tape
- Lift cards
- Fingerprint powders
- Magnifiers

BLOOD COLLECTING MATERIAL

- Rubber gloves
- Test tubes
- Distilled water
- Luminol
- Reagent
- Acetic acid
- Spray bottles
- Spot plates
- Cotton
- Cloth
- Syringes
- Toothpicks
- Saline solution
- Hydrogen solution (three percent)
- Vacuum blood collection tubes with EDTA Orthotolidine

DIGGING-CASTING-GENERAL

- Plaster of Paris
- Rubber/plastic mixing bowls
- Wooden spatula
- Modeling clay
- Shovel
- Hammer
- Dental-impression material
- Lacquer spray
- Electric drill (and bits)
- Screwdriver(s)
- Knife

- Putty knife
- Wire cutters
- Heavy gloves
- Metal retaining bands
- Cotton gloves
- Hacksaw
- Power saw
- Sifters
- Ladder
- Vacuum cleaner
- Hand vacuum
- Vacuum filters
- Tape recorder
- Metal detector
- Extension cords
- Socket wrench
- Portable generator
- Axe
- Prybar
- Portable floodlights
- Pliers
- Gunshot residue test kits
- Rope
- Bolt cutter

Crime Lab Photographs

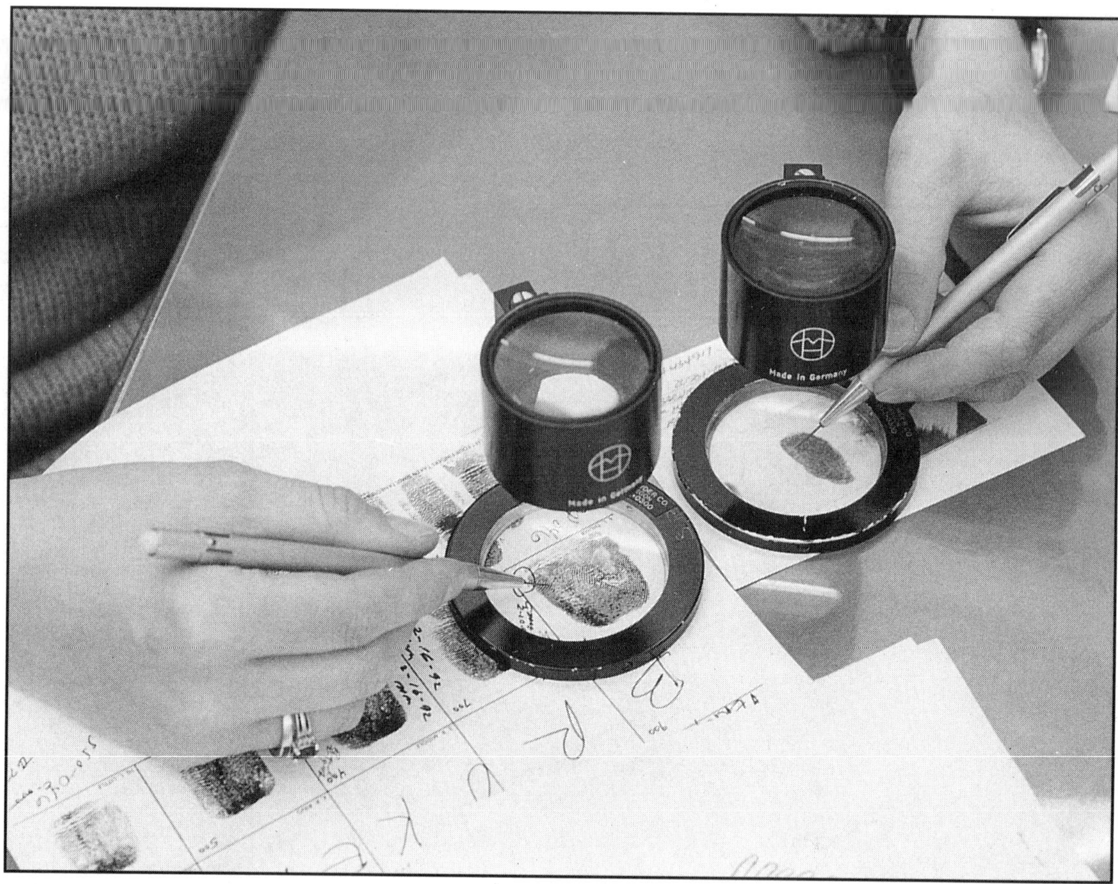

Latent prints are the most common type of physical evidence collected at crime scenes. The term "latent" refers to the prints' characteristic that it is usually invisible to the observer and must be treated with some sort of visualizing agent. This photo depicts an examiner comparing a latent print against an inked fingerprint card. The latent was made visual by dusting fine black fingerprint powder onto the surface containing the latent and then lifting the print by means of cellophane fingerprint tape.

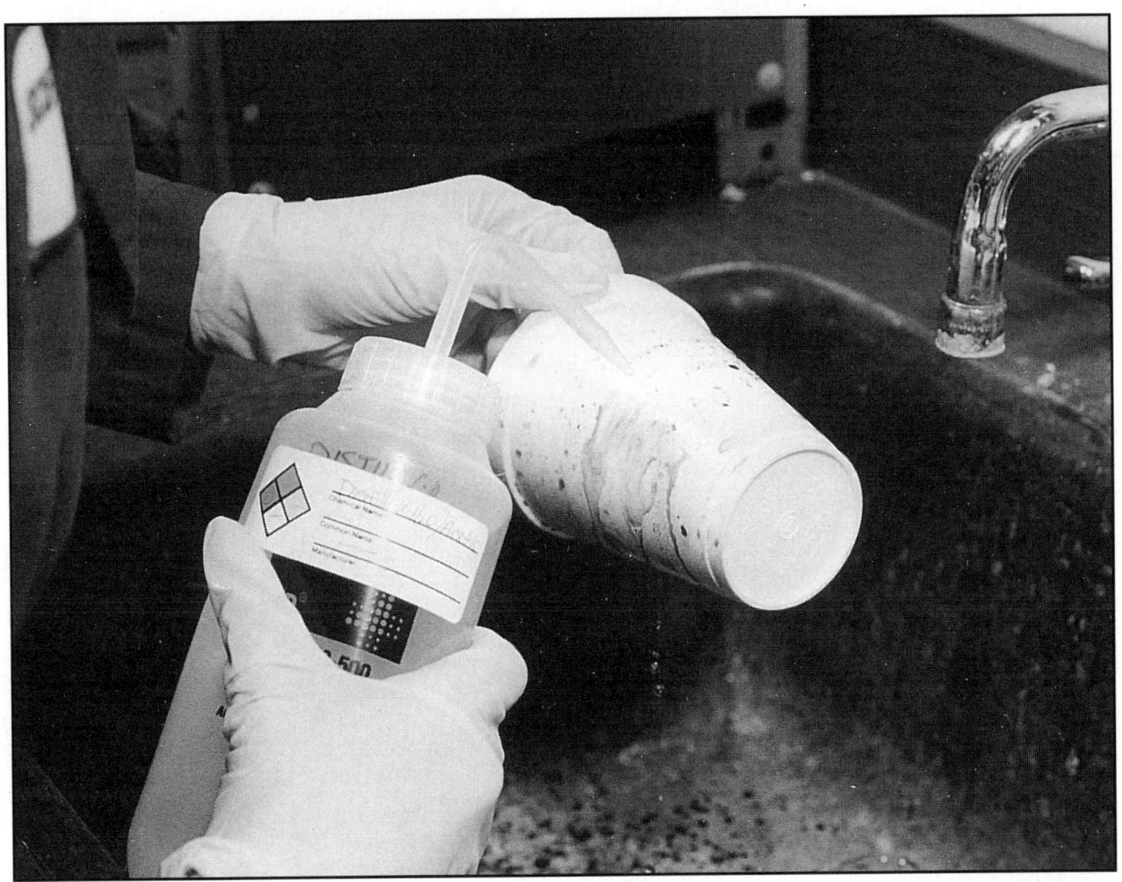

Some surfaces do not lend themselves to dusting with fingerprint powder. There are a number of other ways in which latents may be made visible. In this photo, a fingerprint examiner is rinsing off excess chemicals, from a styrofoam cup. Certain chemicals react with material contained in the print. Such materials may be made up of perspiration, amino acids, fat, blood, or foreign debris. Depending on the nature of the material and the matrix or surface the latent is on, different procedures may be used.

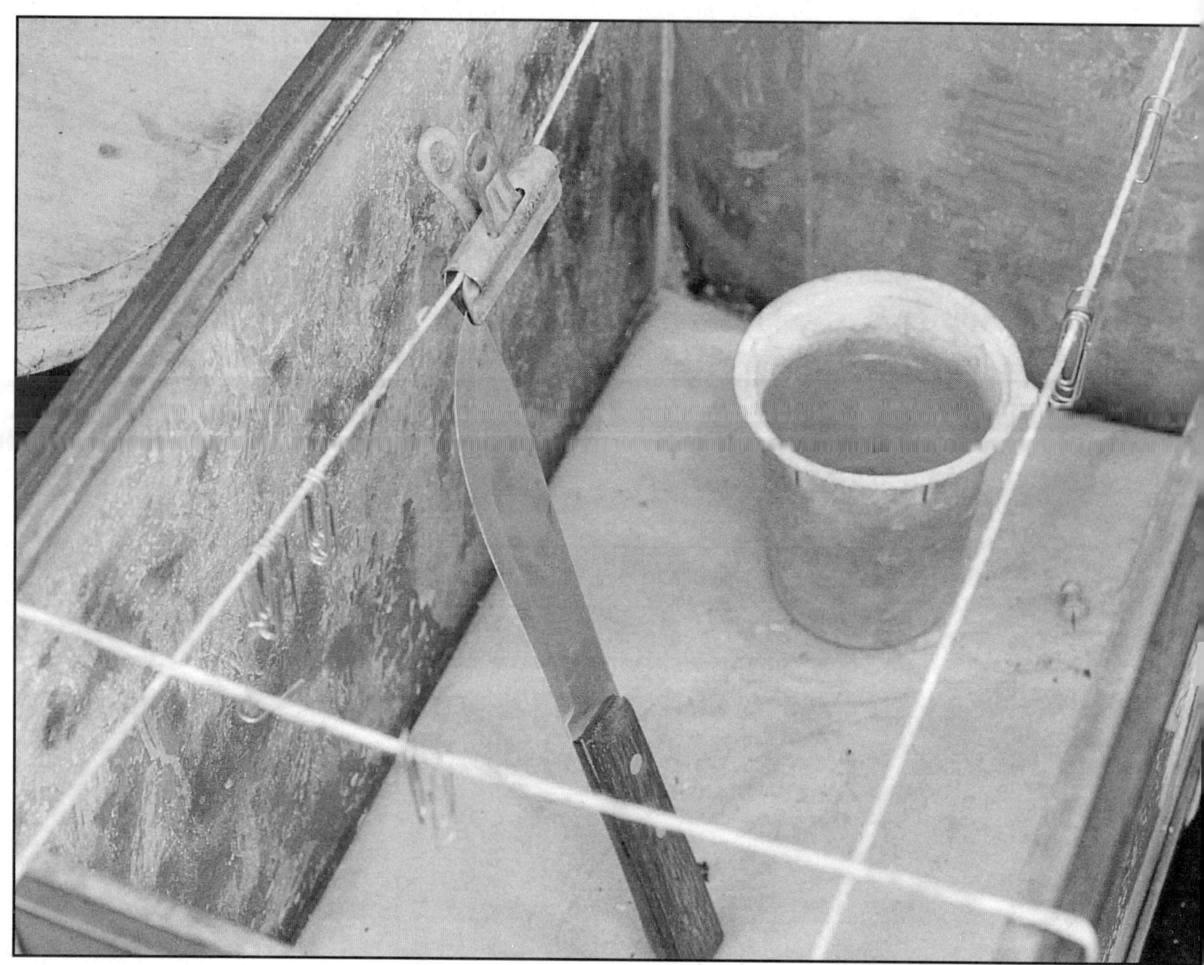

The examinations for latents on smooth, non-porous surfaces is often done using Superglue®, the commercial name for the chemical cyanoacrylate. The item is placed into a chamber such as an aquarium or large-diameter cylinder. A small amount of cyanoacrylate is left along with the evidence and the chamber is sealed. The glue evaporates and is deposited onto the smooth surfaces. If latents are present, the print looks white. It can be dusted and lifted with fingerprint powder, or treated with chemicals that fluoresce when exposed to high-intensity light, such as a laser.

Bullets as well as shell casings can be used to determine whether a specific gun fired a round. In this photo, a firearms examiner has placed a shell casing known to have been fired from a particular gun on the left microscope stage and a shell recovered from a crime scene on the right stage to visually compare microscopic marks made by the breech face and firing pin of the gun when the gun fired. These marks are unique and a match proves that only one firearm, to the exclusion of any other, fired the round.

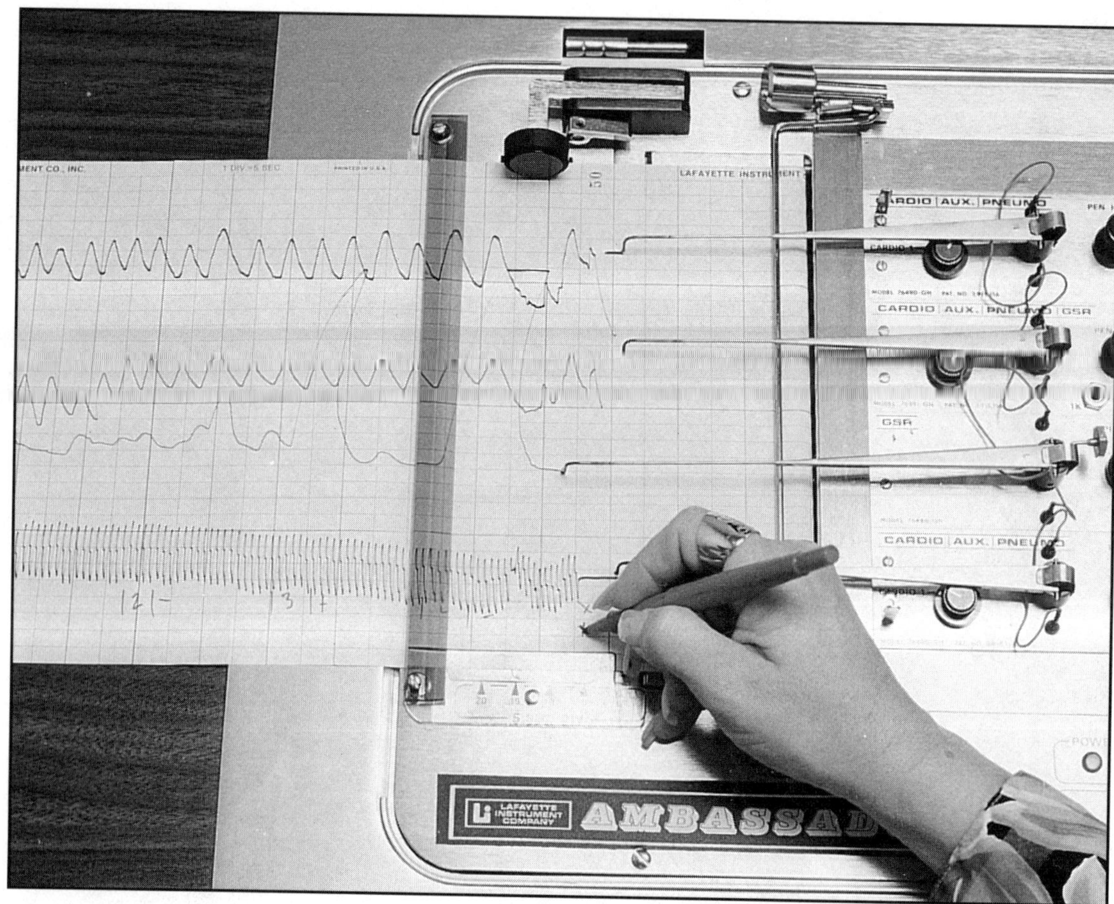

Polygraph units are often housed in forensic-science laboratories. Investigators who are experienced detectives with excellent interrogation skills are selected and trained as polygraph examiners. The term "lie detector" is a misnomer. The polygraph does not detect lies, but rather subtle physiological changes (pulse rate, breathing, and perspiration) brought on by the stress of the questions asked in the polygraph examination. Specific questions are carefully gone over with the subject by the polygraph examiner before the actual test is run. The purpose of the pre-test interview and the actual questioning is to intensify the subject's anxiety, which in turn causes minute, but measurable, physiological changes. These occur only if the subject has knowledge about the crime known only the perpetrator.

Crime Lab: Q & A

Q: Can you suggest the names of poisons that can kill but are difficult to test for?
A: There are way too many to begin listing. I suggest you check the Merck Index, which lists thousands of poisonous chemicals, or the public library's forensic toxicology books.

Q: In the event a murder is committed with a knife and the murder weapon is not found, could the Medical Examiner determine or offer an educated guess about the type of knife that was used and whether it was held by a right- or left-handed person?
A: An autopsy would reveal the depth and length of the wound, offering some indication regarding the size and shape of the weapon and possibly the strength of the individual who inflicted the wound. As for the assailant being right- or left-handed, that could depend a great deal on which side of the victim's body the stab was made. This is not a certainty, only a good possibility.

Q: Back when people still used typewriters, a typewriter could be identified by the wear and tear of the letters that strike the paper. What happens with computers? Can we identify the printer?
A: Believe it or not, we are getting there. It's not one hundred percent, but close, and soon we'll be able to pick out a specific printer just as we can pick out a specific typewriter.

Q: Would fingerprints remain on an object that has been thrown into salt water for say two or three days, and could those prints be lifted if they were there?

A: There are cases in which latent prints have developed rather well on wet items. It depends on what the prints are on—even on the best possible surface, it's a try-and-hope-you-get-lucky situation.

Q: Can a face be reconstructed, like I've seen done on TV and in movies, when most of the actual face is missing or there is only a skull remaining? And if so, how is it done?
A: It's possible, but it takes a lot of skill and workmanship to accomplish it. In the case where part of the face is missing, it would be best if there was a photograph of the individual. When there is only a skull, the first determination would be if it was that of a male or a female. (The walls of the cranium are usually thinner in the male than the female.) When attempting to reconstruct the face of an individual from the skull, it is also helpful to note the existence of teeth and spaces where a bridge or a false tooth might have filled those spaces in order to properly reconstruct the mouth and the jaw as well as the shape of the remaining teeth. Buck teeth or crooked teeth may alter the shape of the mouth. X-rays of the mouth will also aid a forensic odontologist in determining the age of the deceased individual to help in the reconstruction.

Q: If a murder victim has been shot to death, why is it important to take measurements showing how close the gun and the shell casings were to the victim at the crime scene?
A: First of all, the weapon, shell casings, and bullet holes should not only be measured but sketched and photographed as well. This is vital to letting the investigator know not only where the killer was standing but from what height the casings fell and the distance and the angle of the bullets that were fired, which will help determine how far the killer stood from the victim and at what angle the bullets were fired, possibly offering some insight as to whether the victim was standing or sitting when shot and the position and height of the shooter. Any marking on the floor where the weapon fell or was dropped could also indicate how high the weapon was when it was dropped. Traces of wood, fiber, paint, building material, hair, and blood should also be photographed and noted. If a shotgun was used, the pattern of the shot can

tell the investigator a lot about the shooting and help in the reconstruction of the scene just prior to the killing.

Should the victim be holding the weapon, special notice should be taken of the victim's hand and his or her grip on the weapon because the weapon might have been placed in the victim's wrong hand (the victim might have been right-handed but the shot had to have been fired by a left-handed person—something the killer might not have known or noticed or taken into consideration). Residue would also be expected to be found on the victim's hand had the victim fired the weapon.

Q: Could you please explain the actual meaning and the difference between physical and testimonial evidence?
A: Physical evidence and testimonial evidence are one and the same. Both terms mean hard evidence having shape, size, and dimension that can be used in court and is often stronger than the testimony of a witness. Due to a number of decisions pertaining to law enforcement's ability to use statements made by a defendant, law enforcement turned to presenting physical evidence in court as a means of securing convictions. The fact that much of the physical evidence is examined by scientists and expert technicians when presented in court makes law enforcement's case against a defendant much more successful.

Q: Can you give me an idea of what constitutes physical or testimonial evidence?
A: The suspected murder weapon (gun, knife, pillow, rope, blunt instrument), gasoline, blood, bullets, shell casings, fingerprints, buttons, documents, tool marks, hairs or fibers found on a suspect's clothing, possessions stolen from the victim and found on the suspect or in the suspect's home, burglary tools, stomach contents, pills and capsules, charred paper, fingernail scrapings, tire tracks, etc.

Q: What is trace evidence?
A: Trace evidence includes hairs, fibers, anything that can be picked up with an evidence-collection vacuum cleaner that has been designed specifically for the purpose of collecting trace evidence.

Q: What is the meaning of legal evidence?
A: Different jurisdictions have different laws regarding the collection of evidence. By this, I mean that certain cities, counties, and states may have rulings requiring a search warrant or a court order in order for the police to enter a premises and begin searching for evidence, taking blood samples, etc. There are times, depending on the jurisdiction, when the police may be required to obtain a search warrant before even attempting to enter a premises where it is suspected that a murder has taken place. It is best to check with the local prosecutor's office to determine the legalities involved.

Q: Please outline the "chain of custody."
A: (1) Victim's name, possible suspect's name. (2) A description of the item. (3) The name, position, and date of the person collecting the evidence and the subsequent date, name, and position of anyone who takes custody of it. (4) The agency, crime, case number.

Q: Can skin scrapings be considered hard evidence?
A: Although they are "tangible," they are classified as *demonstrative evidence*, which can be linked to the victim or the suspect by blood type and DNA.

Q: How do you determine from what height drops of blood have fallen?
A: Bloodstains and how they fell can tell the investigator a great deal about the relative positions of the attacker and the victim, and in some cases, the severity or power of the impact upon the victim. The splatter depends greatly on the smoothness of the surface. The rougher or coarser the surface, the more the drop will splatter. For example, should you drop blood on an ink blotter, the drop would splatter from a height of sixteen to eighteen inches, while dropping onto a glasslike surface will produce little splatter at one hundred feet. Always figure that the smaller the diameter of the bloodspot, the higher the velocity with which the victim had been hit, whether the victim was shot, knifed, or struck with a blunt, sharp, or pointed instrument. Blood spots can also indicate if there was movement after the attack, and

quite possibly the amount of time that elapsed between the attack and the discovery of the attack. It is difficult to be specific about the size and shape of the blood droppings because each case differs with the surface the blood drops onto. However, as a general rule of thumb, when blood drops from an approximate height of up to twenty inches onto a plain, clear surface, the blood droppings will be circular whereas from twenty to about forty inches, the edges of the blood drop will appear scalloped and large. From forty to sixty inches, the scallops become finer. From sixty to eighty inches the scallops become even finer and have the appearance of a sun ray. When blood hits a wall, window, or mirror, it has pointed ends indicating both movement and direction.

Q. Is there such a science as forensic botany?
A: Yes, there is, and depending on the case, it could help lead to a suspect. Pollen, leaves, flowers, and grass all play a part when footprints are discovered because it is highly likely that the footprints will contain some substance from the area or location where the owner of those footprints has been. Let's suppose a body has been moved to another location after the murder was committed. If footprints are found at the second location, forensic botany can possibly identify the site or general area where the actual murder took place. This could lead to other clues and the identity of the suspect, and should the suspect's sneakers, shoes, or boots be found, the traces on the soles and heels could become evidence. Another example might be the discovering of pollen, grass, or leaves in the footprints that are found. Should forensics find that none of the substances match the area where the body was found and murdered, it could nonetheless tell the investigator what part of the city, county, state, or even country the suspect is from.

Q: Is there a difference between handwriting identification and analysis?
A: Most certainly. Handwriting identification is used to prove or disprove the identity of the individual who is supposed to have written a document. This includes studying the way letters are joined, hesitations noted, styles and shapes of various letters, linked or unlinked let-

ters, writing slanted in one direction or another or without any slant. Often, a left-handed person or a right-handed person will attempt to disguise their handwriting by writing with the opposite hand. But a handwriting expert is hardly ever fooled by this ploy. Also, handwriting experts agree that when a signature appears to be exact in comparison to another signature supposedly by the same party, one signature was obviously traced by a second party.

The Medical Examiner

The job of the Medical Examiner can be crucial to any murder investigation. In most instances, in major cities where the Medical Examiner's Office carries a large daily caseload, the Medical Examiner will send a Medical Examiner Inspector to the crime scene. However, should the homicide be a high-profile case, the Medical Examiner himself or herself will go to the crime scene. In small cities and towns where the Medical Examiner's Office consists of only one person or if a local doctor is doubling as the Medical Examiner, that individual will appear at the murder scene.

AT THE CRIME SCENE: The Medical Examiner examines the body of the victim(s) and gives a description of the wound(s) and the type of weapon that appears to have been the cause of death. (This will later be determined when the autopsy is performed.) The M.E. then offers an approximate time of death by taking the rectal and liver temperatures of the victim.

When the lead detective authorizes the body of the victim(s) to be removed, the Medical Examiner is then responsible for transporting the body to the morgue and for the autopsy and the autopsy report to be provided to the detective in charge of the case. The Medical Examiner must also be available to testify in court if it is deemed necessary.

The Post Mortem: The Autopsy

The lead investigator is required to be present at the autopsy, where he will learn everything the victim's body can tell him about the victim and the means and conditions of the murder.

In the event the victim was killed by a firearm, the autopsy report will include:
• the shape of the wound(s)
• the description of the wound(s)
• the caliber of the weapon used
• the point of entry
• the muzzle impression
• embedded powder and powder burns
• the bullet(s) and type responsible for the death of the victim
• the path and the trajectory of the projectile

In the event the victim was cut or stabbed, the autopsy report will include:
• the type of weapon used
• defense cuts
• hesitation marks
• the number of times the victim was stabbed or cut
• the locations of stab or cut wounds
• lacerations
• the fatal cut or stab wound responsible for death

In the event the victim was poisoned, the autopsy report will include:
• a toxicology examination
• the color of victim's skin, facial muscles
• the type of poison or medication or drug overdose that caused death
• the means by which the poison was ingested, injected, or inhaled
• the approximate time the victim was poisoned, and how long the victim lived before the poison took effect
• the presence of froth at the victim's nose or mouth
• needle marks
• an examination of pills, capsules, or other medications found at or near the scene

Poisons include such gases and liquids as carbon monoxide, benzene, hydrogen cyanide, freon, methanol, arsenic, lead, mercury, hydrochloric acid, sulfuric acid, nitric acid, ammonia, barbiturates, atropine, strychnine, and snake venom.

Death by other means:

There are many ways for a victim to be murdered. Some means are immediately obvious at the crime scene. Yet sometimes what is "obvious" is merely a cover for the real way the victim was killed. A victim's body may have been thrown or pushed from a great height, or the car in which the victim was in went over a cliff. Did it burn on impact or was the vehicle set afire later on by the killer, hoping to disguise the victim's identity by burning the victim? Was the victim shot after having been strangled, smothered, or given poison? Did the victim die from an accident with murder as the coverup or was a murder made to look like an accidental death? Was the victim really a suicide?

In hanging, the hanging groove is examined for distinguishing marks, twisting, knots, width, and type of cord.

Crushing, being run over by vehicle, falling from height, etc. Accidental? Hit-and-run? Often, only the autopsy can reveal the true cause of death.

EXAMINATION POINTS FOR A COMPLETE AUTOPSY:

- heart
- liver
- urinalysis
- spinal cord
- bile
- blood
- gastric contents
- brain tissue
- lungs
- skin
- eyes
- kidneys
- feet
- fingernails
- teeth
- toxicological

The Ongoing Investigation

While the autopsy takes place, detectives attempt to determine the last twenty-four hours of the victim's life: What the victim did, where the victim went, whom the victim saw, whom the victim might have called or was scheduled to meet, what and where the victim ate.

The detectives also notify the next of kin and question them and the victim's friends, business associates, and romantic interests, if any, about their relationship to the victim and any knowledge or suspicions they may have about who might have killed the victim and any possible motives. If no suspect has yet been identified as the probable killer, detectives begin questioning all other individuals who might have had a motive and an opportunity for killing the victim.

Homicide: Q & A

In the following Q & A, the questions were posed to homicide officers who actually work murders, including the crime scene, the interrogation of suspects, the questioning of witnesses, and all the other legwork that goes into a homicide investigation. The question were posed primarily by crime writers.

Q: Could you give me a legal definition of criminal homicide?
A: A criminal homicide is the taking of a human life that is neither justifiable nor excusable.

Q: What constitutes a criminal homicide?
A: Not a simple question that gets a simple answer. First, the victim's death must occur within a year and a day of the assault and the victim must have died of an injury sustained during the assault.

Murder, as opposed to manslaughter, can be broken down this way:
(1) Murder is killing with malice aforethought or with premeditation. The law assumes all homicides to be criminal unless proven to be justifiable or excusable in a court of law.
(2) A criminal homicide must include any of the following:

(a) Premeditation;

(b) The intent to kill or cause bodily harm;

(c) The perpetrator must be engaged in a dangerous act with wanton disregard for human life and must be involved in a felony against a person, as in robbery, rape, aggravated assault, hijacking, or arson. This is known as felony murder.

Q: Is there any difference in where a murder takes place, i.e., what if the body has been moved?
A: A criminal homicide is considered to have taken place at the scene of the act itself, even if the victim died elsewhere. For example, in the murders of Nicole Simpson and Ron Goldman, there was enough blood and evidence to prove conclusively that both victims were murdered where their bodies were found. However, there are many cases where the victim has been shot or knifed and then transported to a deserted location and either dropped or buried there, miles from where the actual act took place.

Q: What is an innocent homicide?
A: An innocent homicide can be either excusable or justifiable. A justifiable homicide is either commanded by law (a soldier upholding his duty, a legal killing by a law enforcement officer, self-defense, protecting the life of another person, or a legal execution of capital punishment as ordered by the court). An excusable homicide is a homicide, justifiable or not, involving criminal intent, such as when a killing is committed by a reasonable mistake or an accident that is not caused by criminal negligence or that of willful and wanton conduct. For example, you are on a hunting trip and suddenly there is movement in the brush up ahead. Not knowing that there is another hunter there and assuming it is the animal you're hunting, you fire your weapon, then learn it wasn't the animal you were hunting but an unannounced hunter you have shot. It was a reasonable mistake.

Q: What is the charge for a murder that is caused by criminal negligence?
A: That depends. In many cases, criminal negligence cannot be the basis of malice for a charge of Murder. On the other hand, should the assailant use a dangerous instrument, such as a weapon (a gun, a knife, a blunt object), it could raise the issue of willful and wanton conduct, which could be considered sufficient to charge that individual with Murder. Or, let us suppose the victim was hit by a drunken driver who claims not to have seen the victim crossing the road. The law considers the vehicle to be a dangerous weapon if not properly driven by a

licensed driver in complete control of his or her senses. If the driver of the vehicle was intoxicated, he was driving illegally and, although he did not have the intent to kill, his negligence in driving while intoxicated means he is criminally negligent. The same would apply to someone driving a vehicle while knowing the brakes were not working, allowing someone to operate a piece of machinery that was not in good working order, or letting someone sail a boat that was not seaworthy, etc.

Q: Are there various types of murderers or is a murderer just a murderer?
A: Yes, there are classifications of murderers, just a serial killer is a special type. Funny as it may sound, one type is considered to be a *normal* killer. We refer to this type as normal because there is no special reason for his killing. He or she is just someone who has no regard for human life. A person taking pot shots at drivers on a freeway would be a perfect example. He couldn't care less about killing someone.

Another type of murderer we call the Temporary Psychotic because this type of murderer suffers great passion or mental illness at the time that the murder is committed.

Then there is the Compulsive murderer. This type is considered to be an individual who is unable to control or prevent his or her own violent, aggressive behavior. A study of the Leopold & Loeb case and the book *Compulsion* will give you a very good insight into this type and how Compulsion came to be a defense tactic.

The Impulsive murderer commits murder because of an irresistible impulse, and there is usually a medical and physiological basis for this type of murderer and the defense that is offered.

The Avenging killer is one who seeks and receives aggressive relief from the violent severing of a relationship.

The Sociopathic killer is one who wages war against society or a specific element of society.

The Addictive murderer is one who commits murder because of an addiction to alcohol or drugs.

The Sadistic killer receives sexual gratification from the actual act of killing his victims.

The Passive-Aggressive murderer absorbs painful hostility until he can take no more and explodes in a violent rage.

There are unlimited motives for murder that would not necessarily apply to any of those murders listed above. Many people kill for profit, revenge, jealousy, fear of leaving their loved ones behind, insurance benefits, or mercy. The motives go on and on.

Q: If a detective catches the call on a homicide but is killed or suspended after the start of the investigation, who gets the assignment, and does the investigation start all over or do the new investigators pick up where the other investigator left off?

A: In most instances, unless there are unusual circumstances, the detective who is killed or removed from the case is replaced by the other lead detective, usually the other detective's former partner. Assigning a completely new team to a running case would be highly unlikely.

Once an investigation begins, homicide investigators immediately begin what is known as a Murder Book. This book will contain every minute piece of information related to the homicide, beginning with the report of the first officer on the scene. It will include interviews with possible witnesses and possible suspects, information, diagrams, statements and reports from everyone involved in one way or another with the homicide, and, of course, everyone assigned to the investigation, including those from the crime lab, the photographers, the Medical Examiner, etc.

The replacement lead detective and the same homicide team would merely pick up where the Murder Book leaves off. After reviewing whatever it contains, they would continue it as they continue the investigation.

Murder has no statute of limitations—murder remains an open case no matter how long it remains unsolved. After a prescribed period of time, an unsolved murder case eventually goes to the "Unsolved Unit," which reviews old cases or picks up new ones as described.

Q: If a homicide investigator should be suspected of planting false evidence, who would handle the investigation of that investigator—Internal Affairs or the District Attorney?

A: In a large law enforcement agency, it would be handled by Internal Affairs or the Internal Criminal Investigation Unit. In a small agency, it might be handled by the District Attorney's Office, especially if there is a possible political motivation.

Q: Suppose there is a twenty-year-old unsolved murder and our protagonist (or someone) is interested in the case. Would the department open up a twenty-year-old case, and if so, what would they do?
A: First of all, remember that there is no statute of limitations on murder. Although a case may still be unsolved and is not being actively pursued, with so many scientific and forensic developments that have come about since the original investigation, it would be like working a new case minus a crime scene. It would be difficult because witnesses may have moved or died, but then again, those witnesses who are still alive who might have had reason for staying silent at the time of the murder might be willing to talk now.

Case in point: Some years back, Dr. Sam Shepherd was convicted of murdering his wife in her bed. The press helped make it an open-and-shut case, and Shepherd was convicted and sent to prison, although he professed to being completely innocent. Years later, interested parties reopened the investigation and discovered that the blood on the sheets, pillowcase, headboard, and the wall behind the bed was, in fact, not the blood of Shepherd's wife. The police had just assumed that it was. Then it was discovered that the corpse's lividity (where the blood settles after death) was not in her back and in the back of her legs as it would have been if had she been lying in bed when she was murdered, as was suspected. The lividity revealed that all her blood had settled in her legs, meaning only one thing: She had to have been sitting or in a vertical position when she was killed and had to have remained in that position for sometime before ever being placed on the bed. Obviously, she had been killed somewhere else—not in her bed, as originally believed. [As this book was being written, an announcement was made after all these years that Dr. Sam Shepherd, although now deceased, was found to be totally innocent of the murder of his wife.]

Q: Could you explain the meanings of and the difference between Corpus Delecti and Habeas Corpus? I'm confused!
A: The legal and literal term "Corpus Delecti" means "produce the body." It does not mean to produce the actual body of the victim. It means to produce the body of evidence to prove that a crime has actually been committed. Sometimes the term is confused with habeas corpus, the word corpus sounding so much like the word corpse. Habeas corpus is actually a legal proceeding instituted by a writ (a court order to a public officer or a private person to do a certain act). This can mean to produce the victim or it can mean "to order a person for a judicial process."

Q: What happens when a local law enforcement agency and the FBI both work on the same case?
A: They usually create a task force and work and exchange information. This is usually done in association with auto thefts, drugs, and vice. There seldom is a local/federal task force in the event of a murder, although a local investigator may travel outside his or her normal jurisdiction to check evidence and follow up on the case. In a few situations, however, a federal/local task force will work together on murders. These are usually cases involving a serial killer who moves from city to city and state to state. It can also happen as a result of a bombing, an act of terrorism, in a city where the murderer/terrorist has been thought to have fled the area, and in the event of a kidnapping/murder when the kidnapper or the kidnapper and the victim have crossed a state line.

Q: If a murder victim's body is found in City X but was murdered in City Y, which police department conducts the investigation?
A: The location where the murder occurred (City Y) would be the actual murder scene, making City Y's police department the primary investigative agency. City X, where the body is found, is called the "secondary scene." In all probabilities, the two departments would work together, with the lead detective of City Y in charge.

Q: Why do they say that the first twenty-four hours of a murder investigation is so important?
A: Because that is when everything is the freshest. It's the time when witnesses recall what they heard or saw before they think things over and start to change their statements. The first twenty-four hours give the police the best opportunity to catch the suspect if one has been identified. They give the police and the crime lab the opportunity to learn where the victim was just prior to the murder, what the victim ate that could lead the police to the hours leading up to the victim's demise. During this period, tracks left by a killer are still fresh. The more time that passes, the colder the case becomes because the killer can flee farther and cover his or her tracks.

Q: What is a defense wound and what is a hesitation wound? Does a hesitation wound indicate that the attacker wasn't sure if he or she wanted to kill the victim?
A: A defense wound or series of wounds are sometime found on the hands of victims trying to shield themselves from attack if it was a slashing attack or someone coming at the victim with a knife rather than just plunging a knife into the victim's back, heart, or chest. Certain cuts reveal that the defendant was trying to ward off the knife attack. A hesitation wound applies to suicides who, in the course of slashing their wrists or cutting their throats, may not have been fully convinced that they wanted to die—thus the "hesitation" wound. Gunshot victims shot at close range may show defense wounds from trying to grapple for the gun, and if the gun is fired at close range, the victim will most likely show powder burns on his or her hands.

Q: Can you tell me something about human remains that have been discovered after a long period of time?
A: The answer to that question would vary depending on where the remains were found. For example, there is quite a difference between a body that has been in the water for an extended amount of time as opposed to one that has been buried in a very dry climate, such as a desert. Then again, a body buried in snow and ice for a long, long time would have a totally different appearance as well.

A body buried in a hot, dry climate will, in most instances, mummify with the body fluids evaporating while the tissues remain in fairly good condition. However, much of that depends on the evaporation of the body fluids. Should there be parts of the body that have not been able to release the body fluids, that part of the body would decompose rapidly.

In bodies taken from the water after having been immersed for a long period of time, the body's fatty tissues develop into a soapy substance called adiocere, making the body very light in weight but inflated and giving off a most obnoxious odor.

A body discovered in snow and ice rarely decomposes, remaining almost in a state of suspended animation. Frozen, the body retains its life-like appearance but, once allowed to defrost, will begin to decompose as any corpse would.

Q: If a murderer commits more than one murder but is not considered to be a serial killer, would this murderer kill again the same way he committed the first killing?
A: I would say that, in most cases, there would be minimal resemblance. However, a homicide investigator with a trained eye might be able to spot something indicative of the learned behavior of the killer that could tie the two murders together and thus lead to the apprehension of the killer who committed both murders.

Q: What is meant by a contact wound?
A: A contact wound is one that results from the muzzle of a gun being held directly against the head or the body of the victim. A contact wound would reveal powder burns on the victim due to the closeness of the muzzle. The term for this is tattooing. In many instances, powder may also fly back onto the hand of the killer who is holding the gun and leave some tattooing on the gun hand of the killer. When the weapon is fired from more than fifteen feet from the victim, only the bullet hole in the victim can be seen.

Q: Is the point where a bullet exits a body larger than the entry point?
A: When the bullet enters a body, the skin is pushed in and perforated,

which in turn stretches the skin of the victim, but once the bullet has passed the point of entry, the skin partially returns to its original form, smaller than the dimension of the bullet. When the bullet first enters the body, it leaves what is known as an abrasion ring, a pinkish rim around the point of entry. The exit wound, in most cases, is much larger than the entry wound and has no abrasion ring. However, what happens to the bullet once it enters the body of the victim is another story, which would depend on how the bullet travels inside the body. Does it lodge itself in muscle, hit a bone and splinter it, continue on, or lodge itself in the bone? If the bullet enters the brain, the bullet could produce an explosive effect and splinter into a number of fragments, exiting in more than one place. Much of what a bullet does depends on the proximity of the gun to the victim and the velocity of the bullet.

Q: What is the underlying cause for mutilation murders?
A: Most mutilation murders are done by serial killers who are bent on mutilating their victims. A non-serial killer mutilates a victim out of passion and rage. There are times, however, when a killer plans or needs to move the body, and in order for the body to fit in a confined space, must chop or cut up it into parts to transport it. Another reason for a non-serial killer to mutilate a body is to grind it or cut it into pieces and bury it in different places in the hope that the remains might be unidentifiable.

Q: What kind of gun is used most often by those committing murder?
A: I'm afraid there aren't any statistics on the type of gun (single shot, revolver, automatic, semi-automatic) used in most homicides. And handguns aren't the only type of guns used to take someone down. Killers have used machine guns, rifles, and shotguns, so there isn't any one preference in the type, size, or caliber.

Small arms (handguns) are broken down into four categories:

(1) The single shot is loaded, fired, and unloaded manually.

(2) The revolver has a rotating cylinder and, depending on the model, can hold anywhere from four to twenty-four cartridges. (A cartridge or "round" is made up of the bullet—the front tip that is fired into the target—and the shell casing, which contains the powder,

primer, and the bullet.) Each time a shot is fired, the revolver's cylinder turns, placing the next cartridge in a position to be fired.

(3) The automatic is a repeater (much like a machine gun), which is loaded with a clip and continues to fire as long as the finger remains on the trigger.

(4) The semi-automatic pistol (which is also clip-loaded) fires one shot each time the trigger is pulled.

Ammunition for small-arms handguns generally are rimfire and centerfire, the ammunition for semi-automatic handguns includes .22 caliber, .25 caliber, .32 caliber, .380 caliber, 9mm, .40 caliber, .45 caliber. Ammunition for revolvers includes .38 caliber, .357 caliber, .41 caliber, and .44 caliber.

Q: Can a superior officer influence or give any countermanding orders at the crime scene?
A: No. The crime scene investigator is in charge and is responsible for the integrity of the crime scene and, therefore, has the right to control everything that happens at the crime scene.

Q: Are newspaper and television news crews ever allowed on a crime scene?
A: No. Although newspaper and television reporters can be very helpful to the investigator, it is the investigator's job to see that no one visits the crime scene other than those working with him, the crime scene technicians, the M.E., etc. The investigator also should not reveal any information to the press regarding clues, the identity of suspects and witnesses, or even the name of the victim until the next of kin has been advised. Newspaper and television reporters can be harmful to an investigation should they release certain information that could later become detrimental to the capture or prosecution of the suspect. Homicide should do everything it can to release only that information which it believes will not damage the investigation, the attempt to capture the person responsible for the murder, and the prosecutor's presentation of the case.

SUGGESTED READING

Practical Homicide Investigation, Gerberth, Elsevier.
Cop Talk, E.W. Count, Pocket Books.
Scene of the Crime, Ann C. Wingate, Writer's Digest Books.
Serial Killers, Norris, Dolphin/Doubleday.
Victims, Barkis, Scribners.
Hunting Humans: Encyclopedia of Serial Killers, Melton, Mcgrath.
Cults that Kill, Larry Kahaner, Warner Books.
Psychology of Strange Killers, J. Reinhardt, Chas. Thomas Publications.
The Mafia Encyclopedia, Sifakis, Facts on File.
Imposing The Death Penalty, Mathom Press.
The Writer's Complete Crime Reference Book, Roth, Writer's Digest Books.
Malicious Intent, Mactire, Writer's Digest Books.
Modus Operandi, Corvace and Paglino, Writer's Digest Books.
Encyclopedia of Modern Murder, Wilson, Colin, Seamen, Arlington House.

The District Attorney & the Prosecutor

The District Attorney's Office plays a major role in any and all murder cases, and although prosecutors do not generally roll to the scene of the crime, they usually will visit the scene prior to trial.

When an arrest is made, the suspect is taken to jail and booked for the crime. The California Code for murder is 187. Should you be writing about a crime taking place in another state, always check to find out what the Penal Code for murder is in that state.

It would be incorrect at this point to say the suspect has been "charged" with the crime. Charges come later, but they must be filed within forty-eight hours of arrest, unless it is on a weekend, when it becomes seventy-two hours (the courts aren't in session on Saturdays and Sundays). The exception to this is when an arrest is made on the basis of a warrant that has been issued by a prosecuting agency. Remember, the police (or sheriff) do not charge the suspect but merely make the arrest on suspicion of murder. It is up to the prosecutor to determine if the investigator has come up with sufficient evidence for the case to be filed and the suspect to be charged. Once the prosecutor has reviewed the case, he or she can dismiss it or have the suspect charged.

Unless the case is a specially assigned homicide, the prosecutor who files the case is not the prosecutor who takes the case to trial. Specialized prosecution divisions such as Hard Core, Major Crimes, and CAPOS vertically prosecute cases.

Hard Core prosecutes gang homicides.

Major Crimes prosecutes complex cases, including homicide.

CAPOS, which stands for Crimes Against Police Officers Section, prosecutes cases in which the victims are on-duty enforcement officers.

FILING

Once the prosecutor has decided to file charges, he or she must decide if "special circumstances" are to be alleged in the murder case. In California, such a charge carries with it the penalty of death or life imprisonment without the possibility of parole. (Death penalty cases are discussed later.) Once a suspect has been charged, he or she is then considered to be a defendant.

The Defendant & the Counsel for the Defense

American justice demands that every individual is innocent until proven guilty. Anyone accused of a crime, such as murder (or any other crime for that matter), must be read his or her rights, or be Mirandized as it is sometimes called.

Anyone arrested for a crime is entitled to be represented by counsel and if unable to afford a lawyer, one will be appointed by the court. And the defendant or the accused can refuse to be interrogated without counsel present. All conversations between the defendant and defense counsel are considered to be privileged.

It is the responsibility of the defense counsel to give his or her client the best defense possible and not to sit in moral judgment of his or her client, regardless of whether the defense counselor believes his or her client is guilty of the crime.

The defense is entitled, under the Rules of Discovery, to be informed about and to see whatever evidence exists against his or her client and to be advised of any and all witnesses that may testify against his or her client. The same is true for the prosecution.

The Courtroom

The Arraignment

After the complaint has been filed, the defendant is arraigned in Municipal Court. There, the defendant, accompanied by his or her attorney, makes his or her plea (rarely "Guilty" or "No Contest" in murder cases), usually, "Not Guilty."

After the arraignment, the judge schedules the defendant's preliminary hearing, which is also heard in Municipal Court.

The Preliminary Hearing

The preliminary hearing is actually a mini-trial wherein the prosecution presents its evidence and testimony in an attempt to convince the judge that there is sufficient evidence providing probable cause against the defendant to send the case to Superior Court for trial. During the preliminary hearing, the defense has the opportunity to challenge the prosecution and cross-examine witnesses, but unless the defense believes it can prevent the case from going to trial, the defense holds back much of its strategy for the main trial.

Once the Municipal Court judge orders the defendant to face trial, the defendant is arraigned again, this time in Superior Court, and once again, enters a plea.

Before the actual trial begins, the defense usually begins filing a series of motions, calling for discovery (the right to view all evidence and to be made aware of all witnesses the prosecution has), and presenting all motions that can help present his or her case or have evidence or even the whole case against his or her client dismissed for lack of evidence or thrown out on some legal technicality.

THE TRIAL

A murder case is always held in Superior Court. There are two types of trials. One is a jury trial (usually requested by the defense) and the other is a court trial where the judge hears the case and no jury is impaneled. In the event of a jury trial, the defense attorney and the prosecutor go through the process of voir dire, the selecting and challenging of jurors, each side seeking twelve jurors they believe will be sympathetic to their side but also supposedly fair and impartial. During this process, jurors can be excused for hardship, cause, or what is known as a preemptory challenge, which is limited to a given number of jurors per side and used when one side believes that a particular juror would be more likely to side with the opposing side. As the jury is impaneled, alternate jurors are usually chosen in the event that a juror must be excused during the trial. If, during the trial, all the alternates have been used and there is need for another juror, a mistrial is declared.

JUVENILE JUSTICE

A juvenile is considered to be a juvenile until the age of eighteen, and is usually tried under the jurisdiction of the Juvenile Court. However, in the case of a serious crime, such as murder, the prosecution can request that the juvenile be tried as an adult, in which case the Juvenile Court can order a fitness hearing. It is then up to the court to decide if the juvenile is fit to be tried as an adult.

A juvenile, however, who is tried as an adult and found to be guilty in California cannot face the death penalty but can only serve life without the benefit of parole.

THE INSANITY DEFENSE

In California, there are two types of trials—those for death penalty cases and those in which the defendant has pleaded guilty by reason of insanity—called bifurcated trials, which come in two parts.

In the insanity defense (the second type of bifurcated trial), the defendant pleads "not guilty" and enters a second plea of "not guilty by reason of insanity." The first part of this trial is to first determine if the defendant is guilty of the crime. The second part is to determine the defendant's sanity.

In the sanity phase, with the usual opening remarks, testimony, etc., the jury must determine if the defendant was insane at the time the crime was committed. If this is the case, the defendant will be sent to a state mental hospital where he or she is held until doctors can assure the court that the defendant has regained his sanity.

THE TRIAL UNDERWAY

The prosecutor is seated on the side nearest the jury box. The defendant and the defense attorney are seated at a table on the opposite side of the room.

The defense and the prosecution make opening remarks.

The defense presents his witnesses, which is called direct examination. Then the prosecution can examine the defense's witnesses on what is called redirect. This can be followed by recourse, redirect, recourse, ad infinitum.

During the above process, both the prosecutor and defense attorney can present evidence (weapon, clothing, medical information, etc.) that is related to that particular witness. As each piece of evidence is introduced for identification, it is then given a number by the judge and tagged. Once introduced and numbered by the judge, the evidence then becomes part of the evidence trail and a matter of public record.

After both sides present their witnesses, the prosecutor can call rebuttal witnesses to refute the statements made by the witnesses for the defense.

When all testimony for both sides is concluded, both attorneys meet with the judge to go over instructions to the jury. This done, both the defense and the prosecution present closing arguments to the jury.

Following closing arguments, the judge instructs the jury and the deliberations, which must be held in secret, begin (occasionally, some juries are sequestered, but this is quite rare).

THE VERDICT

The jury informs the judge that it has reached a decision.

The judge summons all parties to the courtroom.

The jury enters the jury box.

The jury foreperson hands the folded decision to the bailiff, a deputy sheriff in Superior Court, who in turn hands it to the judge. The judge examines the verdict, then hands it to his clerk. In some cases, the clerk reads the verdict aloud; in other cases, the foreperson of the jury reads the verdict aloud.

If the verdict is "Not Guilty," the defendant is released from custody and cannot be tried again for the same crime—this would constitute what is known as "double jeopardy." If the verdict is "Guilty," then a date is set for the penalty phase and sentencing.

THE PENALTY PHASE

A death penalty case in California is a "special circumstances" case. The prosecutor seeks the death penalty against a defendant only in specific limited murder cases.

THE APPEAL

Appeals of Superior Court rulings, convictions, or sentences are made to the California Court of Appeals. The DCA, as it is known, is divided into various districts serving the different geographic areas of the state.

If you are writing about an appellate decision and use the term "sets precedent," remember that legally an appellate ruling does not set precedent for the state. Only the State Supreme Court can do that, and the same holds true for the U.S. Supreme Court. Remember to check the state that your story or screenplay takes place in.

Courtroom: Q & A

Q: Do both the prosecution and the defense counsel always make opening remarks like we see on television?
A: The answer is yes and no. The prosecution almost always makes an opening statement, but the defense may choose not to, saving it all for their closing argument.

Q: Where can I get a look at court documents and the file of a case?
A: A court file is a public record of a case and can be obtained from the court clerk. You can read the file there or you can have it copied for you.

Q: Once a warrant has been issued, how long before it must be filed with the court clerk?
A: Once a search warrant has been issued, served, and the search conducted, it must be returned to be filed within ten days.

Q: What does the term "nolo contendere" mean?
A: It means "no contest" and is considered the same as a guilty plea.

Q: I once saw a movie in which the judge selected the jurors instead of the prosecutor and the defense lawyer selecting them. Does that ever happen?
A: It can happen in California after the passing of Proposition 115, which allows trial judges the option of questioning prospective jurors.

Q: What is the purpose of opening remarks?
A: They provide a roadmap for the jury, so they can follow the aims of both the prosecutor and the defense attorney in trying to prove their case.

Q: Who goes first in presenting opening remarks, and is it done by the

flip of a coin?
A: No, it is not. The prosecution goes first, since it has the burden of proof.

Q: Why is it necessary for the judge to instruct the jury before they begin deliberations?
A: Because they must be instructed about what is the law. A case can be won or lost by improper instructions to the jury.

Q: What happens when a jury isn't 100 percent in agreement in their verdict?
A: The judge may send them back to the jury room, hoping they can still reach a verdict. If, after a reasonable time or number of attempts, they are still deadlocked, the judge must call the case a mistrial.

Q: In the event of a mistrial, does the prosecution start the case all over again?
A: It is up to the prosecutor to decide if the defendant is to be retried.

Q: Can a death sentence be appealed?
A: In California, all death penalty sentences are automatically appealed to the State Supreme Court. Should the Supreme Court not overturn the death penalty verdict, the defendant still has other recourse, all the way up to the U.S. Supreme Court.

Q: What is a "writ of certiorai"?
A: It is commonly referred to as a "cert" from the U.S. Supreme Court wherein the Supreme Court justices decide if they will hear the case. If they do not decide to hear the case and the "cert" is denied, then the Circuit Court ruling stands.

Q: Is there a specific length of time before the death penalty is imposed?
A: No. Appeals can be drawn out for many years, especially in California with its 1978 reinstitution of capital punishment.

Q: Is there any book that a writer can refer to avoid the mumbo-jumbo of Latin legal phrases?
A: *Black's Law Dictionary.*

THE DEATH WATCH

They say, "Let the punishment fit the crime" and "An eye for an eye." Listed below are those states that have a death penalty and their means of execution. Also listed, according to the latest statistics, is the minimum age for capital punishment. If no age is listed, then no age was specified.

Alabama: Electrocution
Arizona: Lethal gag
Arkansas: Electrocution/Lethal injection - 14
California: Lethal gas - 18
Colorado: Lethal injection - 18
Delaware: Lethal injection
Florida: Electrocution
Georgia: Electrocution - 17
Idaho: Lethal injection/Firing Squad
Illinois: Lethal Injection - 18
Indiana: Electrocution - 16
Kentucky: Electrocution - 16
Louisiana: Electrocution - 16
Maryland: Lethal gas - 18
Mississippi: Lethal injection/Lethal gas - 16
Missouri: Lethal injection/Lethal gas - 14
Montana: Lethal injection/Hanging - 10 (but only if trying juvenile as an adult)
Nebraska: Electrocution
New Jersey: Lethal injection

New Hampshire: Lethal injection/Hanging - 17
Nevada: Lethal injection - 16
New Mexico: Lethal Injection
North Carolina: Lethal injection/Lethal gas - 17
Ohio: Electrocution - 18
Oklahoma: Lethal injection - 16
Oregon: Lethal injection - 18
Pennsylvania: Lethal injection
South Carolina: Electrocution
South Dakota: Lethal injection - 10 (but only if juvenile is tried as an adult)
Tennessee: Electrocution - 18
Texas: Lethal injection - 17
Utah: Lethal injection/Hanging - 16
Virginia: Electrocution - 15
Washington: Lethal injection/Hanging
Wyoming: Lethal injection - 16

California is currently considering a death penalty for juveniles as young as fourteen. The federal justice system's minimum age is eighteen, but not younger than fourteen if waived by the Juvenile Court.

Murders That Out

Here's a string of premises that could suggest a story for a television episode, a movie for television, a screenplay, or a novel. They are just notions for you to develop with your own plot twists and turns and interesting characters.

▸ ▸ ▸ ▸ ▸

What medium you plan to write in is important. Each medium requires its own format and structure.

Episodic television calls for a script no longer that sixty to sixty-five pages, sometime even less than sixty pages, depending on how much action is involved. The episodic format may also call for a teaser (Prologue) and a tag (Epilogue).

A movie for television (long form) usually calls for a script no longer than ninety to one hundred minutes, and also may call for teaser and a tag.

The theatrical film may or may not use some sort of teaser or lead-in under the opening titles.

Novels allow the author complete freedom. The author can write a prologue or write a backstory.

I remind you of these formats because how you develop any one of these premises will depend largely on which path you intend to follow.

1.

A Clairvoyant envisions a murder that is to take place. She can describe the location and offer up the vision of the victim as a woman (or a man) but can't see his or her face. As for the killer, she can describe the killer's clothing but not a face because the killer is wearing a mask.

Suggested locations where the Clairvoyant sees the murder happen:
• Ski lodge and ski slopes
• On the water—a bay, a lake, a river
• In the woods, the window across the street, the opposite rooftop, the trunk of a car.

What the Clairvoyant might see:
• The victim's clothing, but not facial features
• The assailant's clothing, but not facial features
• A masked assailant, a motorcycle-helmeted assailant, and/or victim
• The vehicle that the assailant escapes in—model, not color; color, not model; part or no part of the license plate.

Clairvoyant seeks help from:
• The police, who don't believe her
• A reluctant private eye
• A newspaper reporter
• A friend
• A younger relative of the clairvoyant
• A second clairvoyant.

2.

An attractive young woman hires a private detective to find her brother or sister or roommate or husband or father or business partner who has disappeared. The P.I. is unaware that his client is a hit woman using him to track down the person she is contracted to kill.

P.I. protagonist is:
• An incurable romantic
• In need of money
• A big drinker
• Divorced or a widower with one child
• Unmarried

• Taken in by his client's story.

Tracking down the missing person:
• P.I. has an affair with the client.
• P.I. is fired.
• The Client claims to have no knowledge why or who is shooting at the P.I.
• P.I. finds the missing person.
• P.I. learns missing person is not her brother, etc., but the target of the hit woman.
• P.I. believes the story or doesn't believe the story.
• P.I. is about to be killed by his client. Now he knows the truth.
• P.I. and the missing person must now run for it.

3.

A traveling man meets with an accident and suffers amnesia. An attractive woman shows up, claiming to be his wife. Unable to remember anything, he accepts her and goes home with her, unaware she is planning to kill him and collect the insurance on his life. Then the real wife shows.

There are a number of ways to go from here:
• The two women conspire to kill him and share the loot.
• The impostor plans to kill the real wife before she is discovered to be the true one.
• The victim regains memory, and has to kill the impostor to save his real wife.
• The victim decides to kill both wives, hide their bodies, and claim the insurance on both of them.

4.

A deaf and mute person witnesses a murder. The killer doesn't know that the witness cannot communicate what he saw to the police and begins hunting for the witness, who can't call for help. The mute's only choice is to kill the hunter first!

5.

A television news anchorwoman's job is on the line. Ratings are low. She desperately needs something to boost her ratings and secure her job or maybe even get some sort of talk show of her own, like Geraldo. What better way than to ensure the occurrence of a major crime and keep it going than by committing serial murders herself? Then, to make it even bigger, she starts sending weird, threatening messages, supposedly to herself.

Possibilities:
- Station manager secretly hires P.I. to look out for his star reporter.
- P.I. and Anchor Woman have an affair.
- She falls in love with him.
- He begins to suspect.
- She is torn between her love for him and possible exposure.
- She prepares to kill him and blame it on supposed killer she invented.

6.

A cop is falsely accused of murdering his own wife. He is convicted and goes to jail, where he could very well become a victim before his former partner tries to find the real killer, the people who were responsible for framing him.

Possibilities:
- Group of inmates plan to kill him.
- One or two inmates who disliked him find him a fair guy and decide to protect him against other inmates.
- Prison inmate friends learn through grapevine the identity of real killer who framed him.
- He manages to break jail when his partner on the outside fails to produce evidence of the frame or the real murderer.
- Ex-cons on the outside get calls to help him.
- The real culprit found.
- Suppose it was his partner all along?

7.

A Bounty Hunter has his work cut out for him when he searches for an a psycho actor who is a man of many faces turned serial killer.

Possibilities:
• Bounty Hunter is an out-of-work actor and also can use makeup.
• Serial killer real is a pretty boy who can easily pass for a woman.
• Bounty Hunter is discovered with body murdered by serial killer, and he now becomes the hunted while doing the hunting.

8.

A detective with Internal Affairs is murdered by a band of death-squad cops while investigating a mysterious group of cops who are playing their own judge and jury, killing suspects who have yet to be proven guilty. The I.A. continues the investigation but seems to be dragging their feet. The son of the dead officer killed by the death squad is a rookie uniformed patrolman who is determined to find his father's killer and expose the death squad against the advice of a number of his buddies who think he should just turn the other cheek.

Possibilities:
• The head of the I.A. was his father's best friend.
• The I.A. drags its feet because the new head of the I.A. is the head of the death squad.
• A judge is the head of the death squad.
• The girl the young cop is going with is the daughter of a death-squad officer.
• The death squad votes to kill the nosy young cop.
• Attempts are made on the life of the young cop.
• The girl is killed accidentally when death-squad cops try to kill the young cop.
• The father of the dead girl turns against the death squad.

9.

An actor/stuntman and his newly acquired girlfriend are shot at. The girl is killed and the killer is now out to finish the job and get rid of the witness. The actor/stuntman stages a phony death scene to convince the killer it's all over, then, disguising himself, he is free to find out why someone wanted the girl dead and to bring her killer to justice. (This kind of premise leaves the writer wide open.)

- The girl might have been a spy, making the story one of international intrigue.
- The girl was involved in a blackmail scheme.
- The girl knew too much about something or someone.
- The girl was an undercover cop closing in on a case.
- The stuntman finds himself in way over his head.
- The stuntman uses movie-lot buddies to help but has to go it alone at the end.
- The stuntman uses all sorts of stunt devices to trick the heavies.

10.

The Computer that loves to stalk. A computer stalks an attractive young writer who is dead without her computer and could get dead from it, because someone out in cyberspace predicts his next victim after admitting being responsible for having killed a number of women. Soon he'll be coming after her. The trick is, can her computer find the killer computer first?

Possibilities:

- Stalker/killer can break in and e-mail the most grotesque messages and pictures to his victim(s) at any time.
- Female writer calls upon computer genius to help track the stalker/killer
- Attempt is made on life of computer genius for butting in.
- Constant scare tactics by stalker/killer just to let female writer know how close he can get at any given time.
- Female writer calls in police.

• Police assign bright, handsome young cop to help them get lead on the killer and to protect the writer.
• Cop knocked out. Killer is in the house.
• Killer turns out to be computer genius?

11.

New Orleans: Three women with their hearts cut out are discovered hanging from trees in the bayou. The investigators at first believe the three murders all involve voodoo and witchcraft and then wonder if that's what the killer wants them to think.

Possibilities:
• Investigator assigned is white while the victims are all black.
• Second investigator thinks his partner is dragging his feet because he's a racist and doesn't give a damn.
• White partner must learn about voodoo and customs and traditions.
v Black child disappears—possible sacrifice.
• Black partner hospitalized, leaving it up to his white partner to solve the case.
• Voodoo and witchcraft turn out only to be a cover. Victims are killed for other reasons.

12.

The squad had left him for dead back in Nam. The Viet Cong kept him as an MIA. Now he is back and ready to kill every bastard who left him back there to die!

Possibilities:
• Nam in flashback and backstory.
• Killer's own private "Nam."
• Killer returns and is given a big party by his family, but none from his squad is there.
• Squad reads about the return of their MIA squad member.
• Each squad member feels guilty.

• Returned MIA lures them all together with a reunion party.
• One by one they disappear.
• MIA lures each member to his own private Nam to experience what he went through.
• Squad members disappear one by one.
• Last two track MIA to private Nam. Put through hell.
• Conclusion: Discover no one is actually killed.
• Conclusion: All are killed, then he kills self.
• Conclusion: Discovers one went back for him but Viet Cong had already taken him prisoner, so he spares that squad member, who then kills him for killing the others.

13.

The author of a series of successful murder mysteries becomes obsessed with trying to commit a murder himself to actually experience the feeling of becoming a murderer. The question is selecting the right victim and the right place to do in the victim. He then goes home and writes a true-crime "fiction."

Possibilities:
• Author researches various murders, murderers, etc., to determine which one or combination he will become and commit for his true-crime book.
• Author consults his secretary's detective/boyfriend to help him with his research; the cop is unaware he's helping plot a real murder.
• Good suspense as the Author sets about selecting a victim, choosing then discarding those he doesn't want until be makes his final selection.
• His secretary finds strange notes containing the names of real people she knows.
• Secretary tells boyfriend, who thinks she's imagining things until murder occurs and certain things no one but the killer could know show up in the Author's new manuscript.

14.

A detective assigned to a homicide learns during his investigation that his wife was involved with the man who was killed and it's possible she may have been the killer.

Possibilities:

• The Detective destroys or falsifies evidence to keep his wife out of the investigation.

• Detective becomes so infuriated by his wife's cheating that he doesn't care that she may be innocent and sets about framing her, although he learns the identity of the real killer.

• Partner comes to the conclusion she was involved and arrests her, causing a break in the partnership and the detective husband going after real killer.

• Real killer turns out to be the partner?

15.

Every few months for the past two year, following a tip from an unknown caller, another young and lovely coed at the university who'd been raped and murdered is discovered buried somewhere on the 400-acre farm that belongs to elderly, decrepit, and wheelchair-bound Sam Waterson. Each time the police talk to Sam, he claims not to know any of the young, attractive victims, nor has he any idea how they got there.

What the cops don't know:

• The old man is long dead and his mentally ill son makes himself up with a wig, clothing, and makeup to resemble the father he killed and who is also buried on the land.

Motives:

• To get the farm

• To hide the fact that his father ever had a mentally ill son

• To get the Old Man's money

• To hide the killings that his father had learned about

• To conceal the killings his father had done.

16.

A very successful psychiatrist has a little sideline—getting contracts to have certain people killed. The beauty of it all is that the police can't find any connection between any of the mounting homicides, and there's a good reason for that. The shrink is a hypno-analyst who gives his subjects post-hypnotic role-playing suggestions—killing suggestions—and activates his post-hypnotic subjects by a mere telephone call.

Possibilities:

• Police have difficulty in solving the murders as they are unable to connect any possible motive with anyone seen near the crime scene as they (including the hypnotized killer) appear to be very legitimate people with no attachment to the victims, nor do they have any police record.

• Our protagonist detective's only clue (that he gets later on) is the connection of all those near the scene of each murder; each one being a patient of the same psychiatrist.

• Detective's female partner goes undercover and becomes a patient of the shrink, who programs her to kill her detective partner.

SUGGESTED FILMS

Following is a select list of classic films that deal with murder and are worthy of viewing. Although some are based on true crime and others are fictional, they all offer excellent insights into crime drama for the writer and for the avid crime-story fan.

BODY HEAT: A steamy love affair wherein a wife hires a private detective to kill her husband.

THE BOSTON STRANGLER: A film portrait of a true serial killer who terrified Boston for over a year and a half.

D.O.A.: A dark thriller about a poisoned man trying to find his own murderer and the motive for his coming demise before the poison takes effect.

DOUBLE INDEMNITY: A classic story about an insurance agent who is seduced by a deadly woman into insuring and then killing her husband so that they can share in his death benefits. Considered by fans and writers alike to be one of the best crime films ever made.

HALLOWEEN: Acclaimed as one of the most successful independent films of all time, this film deals with a deranged youth who gets out of a mental asylum after fifteen years to return to his hometown to commit murder!

MURDER ON THE ORIENT EXPRESS: An Agatha Christie classic whodunit that follows the exploits of master sleuth Hercule Poirot as he goes about solving a murder aboard the famous Orient Express.

PSYCHO: Directed by the masterful Alfred Hitchcock, this film is a terrifying suspense thriller wherein a young woman steals a fortune and encounters a strange young man and his mother.

THE SILENCE OF THE LAMBS: A terrifying suspense thriller about a mutilating serial killer—a maniac that the police and a behavioral scientist are desperately trying to catch—who another imprisoned serial killer has insight into.

OTHER CRIME FILMS OF NOTE THAT CAN BE FOUND IN YOUR LOCAL VIDEO STORE

Basic Instinct
Blow Out
Bonnie and Clyde
The Client
The Dead Pool
Dirty Harry
Dressed to Kill
Fargo
Fatal Attraction
The Firm
Fort Apache, The Bronx
Gorky Park
In Cold Blood
Internal Affairs
Klute
Laura
Lethal Weapon
The Maltese Falcon
Natural Born Killers
North by Northwest
The Onion Field
The Pelican Brief
Pulp Fiction
Single White Female
The Usual Suspects
Witness

About the Author

Martin Roth has been a television/film writer and producer for more than forty years, and more than 500 of his scripts have been produced. Among the television series he has written for are *Ellery Queen*, *Hawaii Five-O*, *Hart to Hart*, *Barnaby Jones*, *Mannix*, *Night Stalker*, *Ironside*, *It Takes a Thief*, *S.W.A.T.*, *Matt Helm*, *Kaz*, *Vegas*, *The Adventurer*, *Monty Nash*, and, most recently, *Marker* and the TV movie *Voices from Within*.

Although Roth has written comedy and non-crime drama, the subject of crime fascinated him so much that he began concentrating primarily on that genre and soon found himself totally enmeshed in and writing for crime series and films. An avid researcher, he developed professional and personal relationships with law enforcement agencies and officers around the world, making him privy to a huge quantity of law enforcement information and reference materials related to almost every conceivable crime and criminal type, including information on motives, means of mayhem, criminal behavior, and, of course, police procedures and the operations of private investigators.

Roth has lectured on crime writing at the American Film Institute, UCLA, UCSD, and other universities throughout the country.